Primary School Leadership in Context

This book responds to the urgent need to explore how different contexts influence the nature and character of primary school leadership and shows how headteachers in different sized schools shape their leadership accordingly.

The author has drawn on a trilogy of related research projects, which in turn investigated leadership in small, medium and large sized primary schools, and sets out the main features of leadership in each category. An evidence-informed portrait of leadership is presented, drawing on the views and experiences of heads, deputies, teachers and governors. As well as focussing on school size the book considers the following related issues:

- Learning-centred leadership – influencing what happens in classrooms
- Structures and systems in schools – how leaders use them
- Developing leaders and leadership – the importance of building leadership capacity

This informative book sets out in a straightforward way what leaders in different sized schools need to attend to and provides many examples of how leaders do this. *Primary School Leadership in Context* will be particularly valuable to headteachers, deputies and subject leaders in primary schools, those who aspire to these positions, and those who are moving schools in search of promotion. Academics and students of school leadership will also find the book useful.

Professor Geoff Southworth is Director of Research at the National College for School Leadership. He has been a primary school teacher, deputy and headteacher and has conducted research into school leadership over the last twenty years.

D1067138

Primary School Leadership in Context

Leading small, medium and large sized schools

Geoff Southworth

RoutledgeFalmer
Taylor & Francis Group

LONDON AND NEW YORK

First published 2004 by RoutledgeFalmer
11 New Fetter Lane, London EC4P 4EE

Simultaneously published in the USA and Canada
by RoutledgeFalmer
29 West 35th Street, New York, NY 10001

RoutledgeFalmer is an imprint of the Taylor & Francis Group

© 2004 Geoff Southworth

Typeset in 10/12pt M. Baskerville, by
Graphicraft Limited, Hong Kong
Printed and bound in Great Britain by
TJ International Ltd, Padstow, Cornwall

British Library Cataloguing in Publication Data
A catalogue record for this book is available
from the British Library

Library of Congress Cataloging in Publication Data
A catalog record for this book has been requested

ISBN 0–415–30395–8 (hbk)
ISBN 0–415–30396–6 (pbk)

To Ben –
A writer in his own right

Contents

List of illustrations

Figures

Tables

Acknowledgements

This book would not have been written without the financial support of the Teacher Training Agency, which part funded the research into small schools, and the University of Reading, School of Education, which granted me the additional time to complete the small schools study reported in Chapter 2.

The two projects on which Chapters 3 and 4 are based were both funded by the Esmée Fairbairn Foundation. The Foundation sponsored the 'Heads You Win' initiative, one of the most enlightened and generous projects in terms of researching primary school leadership. The 'Heads You Win' project supported the analysis of leadership in successful, medium-sized schools in Essex LEA (Chapter 3). The Foundation also fully funded the research into leadership in large primary schools (Chapter 4). The National College for School Leadership should also be acknowledged for its support in allowing further analysis into some of the data from the large-schools study.

There are also many individuals who should be thanked. First, all the heads, teachers and governors who were interviewed, hosted me and others during fieldwork and who completed the questionnaires used to gather the quantitative data. These individuals provided the material from which the analyses and inter-pretations were developed. I am most grateful to all of them, but especially those heads and their colleagues who made me welcome in their schools and patiently responded to all the questions I asked. Unfortunately, I cannot name them because of the protocols I and my colleagues used to secure their anonymity, but I am forever in their debt and I only hope this book is a worthy reflection of their commitment to their schools and to research.

Thanks are also due to: Paul Lincoln who, as Director of Learning Services in Essex, co-directed the 'Heads You Win' project with me and guided much of the analysis; Dick Weindling who co-directed the large schools project and whose ideas and comments have shaped my thinking about leading large schools; Rosemary Jones at the University of Reading for managing all three projects and making all the necessary arrangements so that everything went smoothly; at the National College for School Leadership, Julie Dennis and Sarah Coleman for their work on the final draft of the manuscript; Philomena Meenaghan for her help with the graphics; and Jill Ireson and Martin Young for their comments on sections of the text.

Part 1

Introduction

This book is both late and early. It is late because attention to leadership in different-sized schools is long overdue. Early because it is the first book to focus on the issue and therefore marks a development in the way we are thinking about school leadership today.

School leadership research has been – and in some ways still is – fascinated by leaders. That is, researchers have studied leaders as persons and the individual roles they perform, often to try to identify the secrets of their success. Consequently leadership research has attempted to find the personal characteristics of successful individuals and then transfuse them into would-be leaders. In other words, there has been a long-standing belief that leadership research should seek out the genetic fingerprints of 'great' leaders in order to create a template for everyone else.

Unfortunately, there are many flaws in this approach. One criticism is that too much emphasis is placed on the leader – usually the head teacher – and that this implies an heroic and charismatic view of leadership. Another problem is that the search for leadership traits is highly questionable. When the characteristics are identified and itemised they often produce a person specification which even a saint would have difficulty matching. Both these criticisms are important, but there is a third which is most relevant to this book. Attention to individuals frequently ignores or obscures attention to the context in which they work. One of the most robust findings from leadership research is that context matters. This is not to deny that individuals are important, but it is to say that so too are the situations they work in. Indeed, leadership is contingent upon environmental and contextual factors.

One characteristic that marks out successful leaders of schools is their ability to understand the contexts in which they operate. In many ways, effective leaders 'read' and comprehend their contexts like texts: they are contextually literate. They look at their schools from different angles, listen to a range of informants and commentators and use as much data as they can find to get beneath the surface of the school and understand it as well as they can.

However, while context includes the school as an organisation, that is not the only setting leaders need to attend to. They need to think about their schools' performance levels, improvement trajectories, their staffs' development needs, their schools' cultures and the communities their schools serve. School leaders should also pay attention to the social and economic changes taking place locally, nationally and internationally and likely to impinge on the lives of the children in the near future. Moreover, in a devolved school system such as that in England, where schools have a great deal of discretion to manage their own affairs whilst at the same time being steered by central government policies and funding streams, head teachers and senior staff need to pay attention to the ebb and flow of educational policy formulation and direction.

Thus context is not a simple phenomenon: it is multiple, blended and variable, because contexts also change over time. A school is not a static institution. Schools change in their climates and cultures over the course of half-terms, terms and the academic year. Staff become tired, while some are absent and some find their particular responsibilities especially demanding for a period of time; new staff need inducting and mentoring; pupils come and go. Pupils also grow and mature over the course of the school year, so that Year 6 children are not the same in the summer term, as they prepare for transfer to secondary school, as they were in the autumn term. Children in reception classes also change as they adjust to school and become accustomed to being 'pupils' and members of groups.

Thus any exploration of context needs to acknowledge that the label covers many things. Moreover, we also need to be aware that it is not just a matter of listing all the ways in which context can be itemised, but of thinking about how the different forms of context combine. It is how the specific contextual elements interact and interrelate which makes each school different from the rest. Expressed another way, it is not only the particular ingredients of an organisation's context that makes a school different; it is also the specific blend of these elements that creates its own distinctive chemistry. Indeed, if few studies have been made of leadership combined with context, there has been a similar lack of attention to the way different combinations of contextual factors combine to create specific leadership challenges and opportunities.

It is the purpose of this book to focus on one feature of context, namely the size of the school. Although there are many other aspects of a school to consider, I have chosen this one because it is an important factor in the primary sector.

Primary schools are the largest group of schools in the English education system and also the most heterogeneous. As recent DfES documents acknowledge, primary schools are enormously diverse in character. They are closely integrated into their local communities, with rural schools being very different from those sited in inner cities. Infant and junior schools are different from all-through primaries, whilst some areas have first and lower schools, middle schools deemed primaries and schools with or without nursery units attached to them.

Although context is recognised as important to leadership and a definer of the character of schools, surprisingly little attention has been paid to it in school leadership research. Writing about school leadership too often describes or prescribes what leaders do or should do in a general manner without acknowledging contextual differences. Thus some of the literature is undifferentiated and indiscriminate. Though studies have been made of leadership in urban areas and of schools facing challenging circumstances, little empirical work has been devoted to leading different-sized primary schools.

If we accept that context matters, then researchers should clearly pay closer and more fastidious attention to it. I have always tried to make it plain that much of my research has concentrated on primary schools and leadership in them. I have done this not to be sectarian but because I want to stress that I respect sector differences and also in order to avoid what might otherwise be an imprecise discussion. This book marks another step along the path towards a more careful and sensitive appreciation of how different contexts influence leadership by examining the variable effects of school size upon leaders.

I should also acknowledge that the focus on school size is but one contextual variable. This book makes only a very modest contribution to an understanding of how contextual factors function and shape leadership. There are many other factors to study, both separately and in the ways they combine with one another. Nevertheless, by making a start I hope that what follows will stimulate attention to other important contextual variables.

At the same time as looking closely at how leadership is enacted in different-sized primary schools, the book also offers insights to middle leaders, assistant and deputy heads and head teachers wishing to move from one size of school to another. If leadership is different in larger and smaller schools, then it would help to know this and to understand how leadership roles are played out in different settings. This book attempts to do this, and I believe it provides readers with the opportunity to examine and reflect on these differences before they move into schools of a different size to their present ones. In this way it should be of interest and value to those leaders considering applying for posts in schools larger (or smaller) than those in which they are currently working.

The book is based upon research I undertook to explore the effects of school size on leaders. I began by studying head teachers in small primary schools. I identified ten successful heads in small schools and visited and talked with them and their colleagues about their schools and the ways they led them. This initial study, though small in scale, was rich in its findings. It also had a powerful effect upon me, because it lifted the lid not just on small schools but on the differentiated nature of school leadership and the impact of size. Consequently I began a follow-up project looking at leadership in large and very large primary schools. As I went about this enquiry with Dick Weindling I was able to make use of the two studies as reference points for one another, contrasting ideas from the first with those I found in the second. This comparative approach was enormously helpful and raised all sorts of ideas and issues relating to school size. It also highlighted the need to look at the intermediate group of schools – those of medium size. So I used an ongoing study into school improvement in primary schools to explore what leadership in medium-sized schools was like. I then used both ends of the size spectrum – little and large schools – to frame comparisons with the middle group. By having two comparator groups I was able to devise a series of questions concerning the distinctions between leadership in them and in these medium-sized schools. This approach threw into relief all kinds of subtle differences.

From these three studies I next identified certain themes which, though common to all schools, played out differently across the three different categories of school size, namely:

- Learning-centred leadership
- Structures and systems in schools
- The development of leaders and leadership.

Learning-centred leadership focuses on how leaders influence what happens in classrooms. It is, for me, the single most important task for school leaders. Indeed, it is the responsibility which marks them out as *school* leaders. A great deal of what heads, deputies, assistant heads and subject leaders do is similar to what is done by leaders in other organisations and employment sectors. However, what is distinctive about school leadership is the way leaders influence the quality of teaching and learning in classrooms. Unless leaders know how to do this and practise it they may not be making a strong contribution to the success of the school as a learning centre. As OFSTED recognises, three things mark out successful leadership in schools: monitoring; evaluating the quality of teaching and learning; and taking steps to improve the quality of teaching. We know a great deal about monitoring and evaluation, but perhaps too little about the third, the steps to take to improve teaching.

The interest I have in learning-centred leadership also stems from a wish to focus on *how* leaders make a differences. For too long we have been preoccupied with whether leaders make a difference. This emphasis has also been at the expense of understanding the ways in which leaders actually do make a difference. The chapter looking at learning-centred leadership begins to examine the anatomy of *how* leaders influence the quality of teaching in classrooms.

The emergence of school structures and systems is an important finding. The fact that previous research has tended to concentrate on leaders as individuals has cast the significance of organisational, curricular and developmental structures into the shadows. In Chapter 6 I try to bring these elements out of the gloom, arguing that they play an important role in ensuring consistency of practice and opportunities for staff and curriculum development. They also play a significant role in shaping the culture of the school.

The theme of leadership development involves a number of important issues. The first is the fact that most school leaders learn to lead simply by being asked to take on responsibility for something or someone. By undertaking such tasks individuals begin to lead and learn how to lead. On-the-job, experiential learning is the commonest and most powerful form of leadership learning. Yet as the size of the school increases so too does the responsibility of the head teacher to develop large numbers of other leaders. Also, the bigger the school, the more deputies and assistant heads should play leadership and leadership development roles and the more subject leaders should be deployed as middle leaders and not as resource managers. Size plays a part in influencing the nature of school-based leadership learning.

These three themes are not disconnected from one another. Running through them is a common concern not only to improve leadership but to enhance a particular kind of leadership. If it is true that schools need more leadership, then we must ask: what kind of leadership do they need more of? From the research underpinning this book I argue that it is learning-centred leadership we need to develop and distribute across each and every school. Therefore the structures and systems and the development opportunities emergent and established leaders need are those which support and sustain learning-centred leadership. In Chapters 6 and 7 I weave this idea into the discussion and show how it can be achieved.

The book is organised into three sections. The first consists of this introduction and Chapter 1. Chapter 1 explains in detail why context is important and then reviews what the literature has to say about school size and how it relates to leadership.

Section 2 covers Chapters 2, 3 and 4. These chapters in turn report and review the findings from the three enquiries I conducted into leading small-, medium- and large-size primary schools.

Section 3 includes Chapters 5, 6 and 7. Chapter 5 focuses on learning-centred leadership. Chapter 6 looks in detail and in some depth at the way school structures and systems influence leadership, while Chapter 7 concentrates on leadership development. Chapter 8 sets out the main conclusions to be drawn from the research and the themes I have identified.

This book shows that size matters. Leadership does differ in the way it is enacted and transacted in schools of different sizes. Given these conclusions, it follows that leadership development needs to be differentiated and sensitive to contextual variables. At the National College for School Leadership we are developing programmes and activities which are as context-sensitive and specific as possible. There are many general and cross-sector issues that school leaders can share and learn about with and from one another. While we must be careful not to over-exaggerate differences, one of the contributions the College is making to the profession is the development of a more differentiated portfolio of programmes and opportunities. This provision aims to meet the diverse needs of leaders at specific points in their careers and to address the particular issues which their schools' circumstances and contexts demand of them. This book illuminates some of the issues for leaders in different-sized primary schools and should help to prepare those moving into leadership in a different-sized school.

1 What we know about school size and leadership

This chapter focuses on four issues. In the first section I explain why context is important for school leadership. In the second, I argue that school size is a significant but ill-defined contextual issue. In the third, I set out the trends in primary school sizes in recent years before moving on to the fourth section, where I report what the literature has to say about schools of different sizes and leadership in them.

Context matters

Research into leadership generally and school leadership in particular shows that context matters. On the face of it this seems an obvious point to make: plainly, where you are has a very important effect on what you do. On closer analysis, however, this idea contains many more subtle aspects.

If we take context to mean the school you work in, then clearly the features and factors that go to make up each and every school will have a part to play in shaping what leaders do. For example, if you are a head, deputy or subject leader in a school where the staff work well together, trust one another and support one another, this will have a bearing on how you operate. By contrast, if the staff do not work together at all, do not share and are forever criticising and attacking one another in public, then this too will shape what the leaders do.

Context is thus about understanding the culture of the school: that is, the way things are done in a particular school. However, it also involves many other factors. The school's performance levels are very important: to be a leader in a school which the Office for Standards in Education (OFSTED) deems to be poor and classes as being in 'special measures' or as having 'severe weaknesses' will dramatically influence the priorities set by that school's leaders. On the other hand, in high-performing schools leaders may have very different priorities. In both contexts 'improvement' will be a prime objective, but the nature of the task involved and the roles the leaders need to play will differ. Thus the school as a contextual setting for leadership affects what its leaders focus on and how they discharge their responsibilities.

Yet context is about more than school culture and performance levels. The school's image and reputation, its community links, the school governors' roles, the school site, plant and buildings are also factors that can influence how leaders work. A school that is overcrowded, has buildings in a poor condition or houses pupils in 'temporary' accommodation, or alternatively has no playing field or hall large enough to accommodate all the pupils at any one time, will find that such elements shape the way it functions.

Although I could continue to itemise the factors that go to make up a school's context, that is not my intention here. Rather, what I want to stress is that a range of factors is at work in any one context; next, to suggest that these relate and interrelate with one another; and, third, that they each – more or less – influence leadership. Context is thus simple and complex: simple in that the school is the obvious arena for leaders' work; complex in the range and scale of multiple and variable factors which both separately and together constitute the school. It is within this notion of complexity that the subtleties of context lie.

The idea of context has spawned a number of leadership theories, typically called contingency or situational theories. Hersey and Blanchard (1982) argue that leadership varies according to the maturity of the followers. In other words, not only do leaders' actions matter, but so too do those of the followers. Schools are staffed by adults with varying levels of maturity, and different leadership behaviours may be required for different people. Some individuals may be highly competent and experienced in the tasks they are responsible for; others less so. Moreover, when a person is asked to undertake a new task they may not – in role terms – be very mature in their new role. Therefore when leaders delegate they may need to take into account how experienced and mature the person to whom they are delegating is in terms of meeting the requirements of the task.

This notion of maturity has less to do with the age of an individual – although this can sometimes be a factor – than with their experience relative to the task or tasks they are undertaking. All heads in their first year of their first headship are, in this sense, immature, as are deputies, subject leaders and teachers in their first year of occupying their posts. The issue is how mature or immature individuals are in their particular *roles*. For these reasons there is a growing interest in career development and stages of headship (Weindling 1999), as well as in mentoring, supervision and coaching. It appears that everyone has an early years stage as well as middle and later years ones, in role. The challenge is not so much knowing this as appreciating and diagnosing how quickly individuals 'move' through the various stages. This process of role maturation brings into focus two other points: the fact that this process is individualised, and that it is dynamic.

The discussion has already raised a number of important points about context, but the last one, regarding its dynamic character, is worth dwelling on a little more. Contexts are not static. Schools can and do change their perform-ance levels: staff come and go, mature and gain experience, increase or lose motivation, and energy levels shift over time. Stakeholders' perceptions change, the building can be renovated or left unattended for a while – the catalogue of how the contextual factors alter is extensive. What this means for school leaders is that they need to able to detect these subtle shifts. Leaders need to be good diagnosticians. They should be able to 'read' the school like a text. In my experience, effective heads have a highly developed 'contextual literacy'. They know from the inside – from their close-up knowledge and their dealings with all who form the school – what the school is like this week, this half-term, this term and this school year. As others have said: 'Productive leadership depends heavily on its fit with the social and organisational context in which it is exercised . . . Outstanding leadership is exquisitely sensitive to the context in which it is exercised' (Leithwood, Jantzi and Steinbach 1999: 3–4).

If one implication of contexts being dynamic is sensitivity on the part of leaders to the school's situation, another is that contexts change over time. That we live and work in times of increasingly rapid change – educational, economic and social – is now a cliché. However, it does mean that leadership also has to change. It has to take account of the developments wherever they unfold and to respond accordingly.

Thus context matters because it influences leadership; it is multi-factorial and the factors themselves are variable. Moreover, these multiple, variable factors interrelate in numerous ways, making a school's context changeable. Thus context is differentiated and dynamic.

Given this portrayal of context, there are two further points to make. So far I have defined context in terms of the school. I now want to expand this definition. While the school as an organisation is the main focus of a school leader's contextual awareness, it is not the only one. Increasingly in devolved education systems we need to recognise the national – and sometimes international – dimensions of context. If we think of the school as the micro level of context, then the national educational scene – which incorporates the DfES, policy legislation and initiatives and governmental and non-governmental agencies' influence (e.g. OFSTED, QCA, TTA, NCSL, GTC) – represents the macro level. In between – the mesa level – are local education authorities, diocesan bodies, regional agencies and the local communities that schools serve. These three levels are also nested, with each having implications for the other two. Furthermore, while the micro level should be the most dominant of the three, in terms of how much attention it absorbs, this is not to discount the other two. Indeed, in the past two decades the macro level has become a more active and influential factor than ever before. Curricular instructions, assessment arrangements, inspection requirements are just three examples of this influence. Others are funding opportunities, the creation of new networks and communities of practice, and opportunities to learn with and from best practice across the country and beyond.

The second point about context is that the size of the school is an important factor. Much of the discussion in this section suggests that the bigger the school the greater the contextual complexity there will be. While this is true, it is not the whole picture. Size does matter; but not always in obvious ways, as the next sections aim to show.

Size matters

Although many factors affect the school as a context for leadership, its size is a major one. The larger the school, the more children and staff there are. The more people there are, the more they need to be managed.

School size has long been recognised as important. Head-teacher and deputy-head salaries were once strongly linked to school size: the larger the school, the more the head was paid. This link still exists today, although other factors are now taken into account in determining salaries.

The general assumption is that the larger the school, the more there is to manage and the greater the levels of responsibility of senior staff. While this simple association makes sense, there are two difficulties with it. First, it may exaggerate size effects, possibly at the expense of smaller schools, which are presumed to be 'simple' places to lead. As will become apparent in later chapters of this book, this outlook is not very accurate. Second, the assumptions about size are relative ones. They are based on 'larger than' and 'smaller than' thinking, often without any clarity about what constitutes 'small' or 'large'.

School size is a surprisingly imprecise topic in educational debate and research. There are several and differing notions of what constitutes a small or large school in this country. Moreover, international comparisons are sometimes very difficult because in some systems – such as those of Singapore or Hong Kong – 'large' means over two thousand pupils, even in the primary sector. This is a classic example of a contextual variable, school size, being itself a contextualised phenomenon since what constitutes 'small' or 'large' depends on the norms of the particular system.

In England, a small school is usually taken to mean one with up to a hundred children on roll (full-time equivalents or FTEs). 'Large' is less well defined but usually applied to those with 401-plus children on roll. However, these parameters also introduce other ones, particularly in the case of the very small school, generally one with fewer than fifty pupils (FTEs) on roll. These boundaries, though, are arbitrary ones. They also do little to frame what is meant by medium-sized schools. Are they all schools with between 101 and 400? Well, they could be, but as such they form the overwhelmingly largest category of schools. This grouping of 101–400 pupils covers those with less than one form of entry to ones with over two forms of entry. How many 'forms' or teaching classes a school admits has a strong bearing upon how it is organised and staffed, as any teacher in a one-form school recognises on moving to a two-form school or vice versa. Also, schools with less than one form of entry and those with two-and-a-half forms of entry (or one-and a-half) are ones that frequently have to organise both single-age and mixed-age classes simultaneously. It is far from easy to do this, and the challenges posed by such numbers are often considerable. In other words, to say that medium-sized schools are those which are neither 'small' nor 'large' is to create an undifferentiated middle-order group, which masks some specific and difficult features.

It seems, therefore, that while school size makes a difference, it is often defined in an arbitrary way. School size takes little account of how many forms or classes schools use to admit and organise pupils into, and, within the basic categories of small, medium and large, it is not differentiated. These are important weaknesses in the way the education system uses the concept of size as a contextual variable. Size is recognised as a factor, but has not been explored beyond that.

Nevertheless, given the importance attached to school size, a start has to be made somewhere in moving from an undifferentiated way of thinking about schools and leadership towards a more sophisticated understanding. Moreover, school sizes do not stay the same. They change as pupil rolls rise or fall, either because of macro factors such as birth rates and population trends or due to local factors such as the popularity of the school or of neighbouring ones. The next section focuses in some detail on primary-school sizes in order to identify emerging trends.

Recent and contemporary trends in primary school size

The table below shows the numbers of primary schools and their sizes over the last ten years. The total number of schools over this period has fallen, from nearly 19,000 in 1992 to almost 18,000 in 2001. The two groups of schools which have been most affected by this decline are those with up to a hundred children on roll, which shrank from 3,548 in 1992 to 2,711 in 2001, and those with between 101 and 200 children on roll, which decreased in number from 6,329 in 1992 to 5,333 in 2001. Schools with between 201 and 300 children have also decreased in number, but not as much as the two categories below them.

By contrast, the other size categories have all increased. Schools with 401–500 children on roll grew from 679 in 1992 to 1,269 in 2001. Also, the total number of schools with over 601 children increased from forty in 1992 to 138 in 2001. In 1992 there were no schools with over 801 children; by 2001 there were eleven. These figures can be summarised in three ways. First, there are fewer small schools and more larger ones. Second, although there are fewer schools today than formerly, schools generally are becoming larger. Third, we now have a group of primary schools which are larger than ever before.

Indeed, though the figures shown in Table 1.1 do not necessarily impute this, further enquiries into DfES statistics about school size suggest that we are close to – or already have – a thousand-place primary school somewhere in the country. This is because the figures logged here are based on a January census date and some schools will have another intake of pupils in April, after the Easter break. In the case of three- and especially four-form entry schools these will add an extra hundred or more children to the roll.

Probably two reasons explain the trends in school size over the ten years covered by Table 1.1. First, in the early 1990s there were a number of school closures, with small rural schools under the most threat. The closure of village schools accounts for the decline in the number of schools with fewer than a hundred children and in those with between 101 and 200.

Second, during the period covered by the table many amalgamations of schools have taken place. Typically, separate junior and infant schools have been combined to form a single primary school. Also, some primary schools have been amalgamated to form a single school, and sometimes this has involved two or three schools being put together. Consequently, the newly amalgamated school has become a much larger unit than those that preceded it. Certainly, the number

Table 1.1 Number of primary schools by size

Primary and middle deemed primary Number of schools by size	Year						
	2001	2000	1999	1998	1997	1996	1995
Up to 100	2,711	2,701	2,716	2,745	2,824	2,956	3,111
101–200	5,333	5,263	5,196	5,254	5,344	5,450	5,582
201–300	5,684	5,833	5,941	5,983	6,014	6,000	6,021
301–400	2,669	2,729	2,763	2,776	2,760	2,700	2,621
401–500	1,269	1,256	1,238	1,204	1,123	1,063	950
501–600	255	244	257	245	240	226	207
601–700	125	109	103	86	69	68	46
701–800	12	15	13	15	15	15	11
801–900	11	8	7	4	3	2	2
901-plus	0	0	0	0	0	0	0
Total	18,069	18,158	18,234	18,312	18,392	18,480	18,551

Primary and middle deemed primary Number of schools of size	Year			
	1995	1994	1993	1992
Up to 100		3,230	3,390	3,548
101–200		5,879	6,094	6,329
201–300		6,001	6,050	6,022
301–400		2,511	2,367	2,176
401–500		841	744	679
501–600		168	134	132
601–800		52	48	40
801–900		1	1	0
901-plus		0	0	0
Total		18,683	18,828	18,926

Source: DfES (2002).

of schools with over 401 pupils on roll has grown as a result of the amalgamation process.

Schools with over 401 pupils on roll are generally classified by practitioners as big organisations within the primary sector, yet the truth is that it is schools with more than 601 pupils which constitute the very largest ones. Those with between 401 and 600 children may be large, but it is the group with 601-plus pupils that warrant the title 'very large'. Furthermore, the upsurge in larger schools means that although they are increasing in number we know relatively little about leading and managing them. They are a relatively new phenomenon and as such have been little examined.

In particular, we know little about the way they are led and managed. The particular development needs of the senior staff have not been identified: thus we know too little about how to prepare senior staff to lead such schools.

Furthermore, given that it is the case that most of these large and very large schools are located within metropolitan areas, it follows that a good proportion of them will encounter many of the challenges associated with inner cities, disadvantaged communities and poverty. In other words, heads and deputies in large schools have to create the structures, systems and conditions to ensure their large organisations work efficiently and effectively, and a substantial proportion of them are required to do so in very challenging circumstances. In short, there is a particular need to investigate leadership in very large primary schools.

Literature review

A search through national and international databases, journals and other sources showed that while it is comparatively easy to find material on small schools, work on other-sized schools is much harder to find. Small schools have clearly become a special group in ways that medium-sized and larger ones have not. To some degree this is to be expected. Medium-sized schools are not 'unusual' and can be presumed to be covered by all reports and research, whereas the other two sets of school sizes are different and thus 'exceptional'. Also, small schools have been treated as special cases for some time, at both policy and practice levels.

Small primary schools have received enhanced financial support for many years. On a unit-cost basis some of them are seen as not financially viable, but on other grounds they are nevertheless needed and valued so that local authorities give additional funds to maintain them. With the advent of local financial management of schools the formula funding for them was supplemented by additional grants to ensure their existence. Yet financial viability is only one example of small schools being accorded special status; rural issues and the distances young pupils have to travel to attend a relatively local school are two more. Many local communities have fought to avoid the closure of small schools, and a large number of these campaigns have been successful. They have also given rise to numerous small-school lobby groups as well as professional organisations to represent and protect their needs.

What was unexpected in my searches through the literature was that so very little seemed to have been written on large primary schools. They may be an exceptional category, but they have not been researched. Thus there is a dearth of publicly available information about them, and what is known about them largely resides in practitioner experience.

For these reasons, then, what follows in this section is mostly a review of what we know about small schools. However, the evidence base also includes some references to large schools because they are often part of the small-school debate. There are a number of protagonists who argue *for* small schools by arguing *against* large schools. In short, the 'Small is beautiful' lobby also use the 'Big is bad' argument.

A considerable body of international research exists into small schools. My searches produced studies which reported on small schools in a number of countries, including: Australia, Canada, England, Greece, Iceland, New Zealand,

Scotland, Sri Lanka, Sweden, the USA (the Appalachians, Alaska, Nebraska, Texas) and Wales. Other studies referred less specifically to areas of South America, the Caribbean countries and rural Africa.

While there is a great deal of material, it is generally concerned with two broad sets of related issues:

- Viability
- Educational effectiveness.

Viability concerns were demonstrated by articles focusing on the following topics: sustainability; school closures and survival concerns; cost-effectiveness and value for money; the impact of national and/or local policies on small schools; ways of overcoming the perceived disadvantages of remoteness and isolation (e.g. twinning, clustering, federations, networking). *Educational effectiveness* concerns largely covered such issues as: curricular provision (manageability, coverage, breadth, the implementation of national reforms), school-size effects on achievement; and mixed-age classes of pupils.

These two sets of issues are both constant in the literature and continuing. For example, following the completion of the first four-year cycle of inspections of schools in England (1994–8) by the Office for Standards in Education (OFSTED), inspectors used the data to compare the achievements and quality of education of small schools with those of larger ones. Small schools were defined as those with fewer than a hundred pupils on roll.

The inspectors opened their comparative report by noting that bald comparisons between the two groups of schools are problematic since the majority of small schools are to be found in relatively affluent areas with above-average socio-economic indicators. By contrast, many large and very large primary schools are located in urban centres and thus face the challenges of city life, including poverty and deprivation. The inspectors found that small schools were strongly represented among the hundred top performing schools (in English, mathematics and science tests) between 1996 and 1998:

> A significantly greater number than might have been expected on purely statistical terms have been in the top 100 each year . . . By contrast, there was also a higher than expected proportion of very small schools in the lowest scoring schools between 1996 and 1998.
>
> (HMI 1999)

Though the inspectors do not elaborate on these findings, it looks on the face of it to mean that small schools tend to be either very good or rather weak. In some ways this may be a reflection of the staffing circumstances of such schools. A school with fewer than a hundred pupils on roll is likely to have three or four teachers as well as a higher number of classroom support staff. Where the three or four teachers form a highly effective team and where this is well led by the head, these teachers are likely to be able to produce high-quality standards and results. Alternatively, where a team of this size includes weak teachers, these will have an adverse effect on the school's performance. In other words, the relatively small number of teachers makes these schools more dependent on individual teacher effects than is the case in very large schools. A poor teacher in a small school may well be responsible for the whole of Key Stage 1; thus their influence on the end of Key Stage results will be marked.

Small schools were judged by the inspectors generally to provide the full range of knowledge, skills and understanding required by every subject in the National Curriculum. Moreover, with the exception of the provision for under-fives, the curriculum of small schools is generally at least as broad and balanced as that of larger schools (HMI 1999).

Inspectors also judge the quality of leadership and management in schools. Of these matters the inspectors said that head teachers of small schools provided clear educational direction for their schools, although in line with schools in general 'there are weaknesses in the leadership in about one school in seven' (HMI 1999). Furthermore:

> Good management and good teaching are, understandably, the two most significant characteristics of successful small schools. These two character- istics are uniquely combined in the role of the small school head so that his or her influence is a more than usually important factor in determining the quality of the school
>
> Where the head is effective in both the teaching and the management roles, a virtuous circle of benefits accrues to the school: change and develop- ment can be achieved more quickly, the head is able to lead by example with any new initiative and is well placed, from first hand knowledge, to assess priorities for training and spending. This circle can easily be broken, however; a weak or absent head can quickly trigger a downward spiral with consequent loss of morale and reduced quality of education.
>
> (HMI 1999: 16)

The inspectors concluded that the head of a small school is of paramount import- ance to that school's success because of their more than usually direct influence on the quality of teaching and standards achieved.

Overall, the inspectors say of small schools that higher unit costs notwith- standing, 'a good case emerges for the place of small schools in the education system as a whole when the quality of their educational performance is added to the broader contribution they make to their communities' (p. 16). Such a conclusion supports earlier research which showed that small schools are not significantly different from their larger counterparts in the content of their curriculum and in the manner of its teaching (Galton and Patrick 1990).

The English inspectors' comments are congruent with research in North America. Cotton's (1997) review of research into school size, climate and student performance deals with whether small schools are better than larger ones. How- ever, the review is complicated by the fact that researchers and educators in the

United States have not agreed what constitutes a small or large school. Cotton's summary of findings in small schools suggests that:

- Academic achievement is at least equal – and often superior – to that of large schools;
- Student attitudes toward school are more positive;
- Student social behaviour is more positive;
- Levels of extra-curricular participation are much higher;
- Students have a greater sense of belonging;
- Teacher attitudes to their work and their administrators are more positive;
- Students and staff generally have a stronger sense of personal efficacy.

(Cotton 1997: 12–14)

Interesting and important as these findings are, they do not tell us explicitly whether and how principals of small schools influence such outcomes. Moreover, the studies my searches revealed tend to dwell on the challenges of being a leader of a small school and not on what makes such people 'successful'. For instance, Dunning (1993) focuses on the 'double load' problem of the teaching head. The concept of heads of small schools carrying a 'double load' was first expressed by the Gittins Report (1967) which focused on primary schooling in Wales where a third of all schools then had fewer than a hundred pupils on roll. Dunning used the notion to examine how educational reforms had impacted on the double load. He observed that teaching heads in small schools had experienced an expansion of their responsibilities. Teaching heads are required to demonstrate a much more sophisticated technical competence in their teaching, while dealing with the same teaching load and new management commitments which are as demanding as those of non-teaching heads in larger schools (p. 82).

Dunning essentially makes two points. First, that neither the special circumstances of small school heads, nor those of the schools they manage have usually attracted much in way of sympathetic attention on the part of reforming politicians or central administrators (p. 79). Second, despite the early identification of the problem of the 'doubly loaded' teaching head, thirty years later the bipartite role remains a characteristic phenomenon of most small primaries, and little has been done to alleviate the 'demanding task' which Gittins (1967) recognised teaching headship to be (p. 80). Given all the reforms that have occurred since then, it is questionable whether heads of small schools should still be expected to work under many of the 'double load' factors that were recognised as major encumbrances so many years ago (p. 87).

These points are echoed in two other studies. Hayes (1996) interviewed six primary heads and found that these individuals were attracted to small-school headship because it offered the opportunity to: go on teaching; be their own boss; fulfil a vision; and 'make a mark' (pp. 381–3). However, the realities of headship were such that even the satisfaction gained through continued interaction with children was threatened by the pressure of work. After a time in post, each head accepted that it was impossible to maintain high standards in every area of the job (p. 386). Despite their shared belief concerning what a small-school headship could offer, they had to concede that they were unable to cope with its many demands.

Hayes then explores what this meant for the heads and argues that in trying to achieve success they were also obliged to hide their shortcomings from parents and other stakeholders outside the school. In fact, they worked so hard to conceal these that they sometimes became exhausted. This exhaustion in turn created dissatisfaction due to fatigue and a diminished ability to cope. They then worked even harder to restore their elusive sense of success until they became unable to offer anything more to the job (p. 387). According to Hayes, they felt good about themselves only when they did everything well, but the strain of doing everything well reduced the extent to which they experienced a sense of self-esteem. Feeling positive about themselves as teachers became increasingly difficult; the heavy demands of being a teaching head meant they sometimes had to sacrifice a central aspect of their professional identity – being an effective teacher – in order to cope with the managerial side of the job (p. 388). Thus, Hayes' analysis takes thinking about the 'doubly loaded' head beyond previous studies. He argues that the workload pressures and expectations can be so acute that they become a source of professional strain and personal dissatisfaction with one's professional self. This interpretation is interesting because it suggests that it is as much the expectations the heads have of themselves as the actual pressures of the job which are the source of the dissatisfaction. This may have implications for the training, development and – in particular – the support needs of heads of small schools.

Waugh's (1999) study of eleven heads aimed to examine how head teachers in primary schools of different sizes responded to educational change. All the heads experienced a conflict between their desire to teach and the need to undertake administrative duties (p. 22). Yet this was experienced more strongly by the small-school heads than by those in larger schools. This finding is an important one. It is too simplistic to assume that it is only heads of small schools who struggle to resolve the perceived conflict between teaching and administration: heads in medium- and larger-sized schools also find it a challenge. The issue for small-school heads is that they appear to experience the conflict in a relatively stronger sense. It may well be the case that this issue deserves more detailed and closer examination than has so far been achieved.

My own research with head teachers suggests that, while Waugh is probably right, the pressures of teaching and administration for heads in medium-sized and larger schools warrant further analysis. Indeed, anecdotal evidence from heads of medium-sized schools suggests that other factors are at work which make this issue problematic for them. Heads in small schools who have a class teaching commitment obviously feel their responsibility for that class very strongly and experience any interruption to or distraction from their teaching most keenly. However, many heads of schools with between a hundred and 250 pupils on roll also find managing the dual demands of administration and teaching across the school a challenge. Furthermore, as the need for classroom observation and monitoring has grown, so too may the pressures on heads of these middle-band schools.

Returning to Waugh's study, the heads of small schools tended to maintain that they had insufficient time to manage their schools properly, given their heavy teaching loads. As one respondent said: *'When I grow up I want to be a head teacher.'*

He did not see himself as a head teacher at that moment, but rather a *'class teacher and an administrator'* (p. 30).

In common with the inspection evidence Waugh states that heads of small schools have certain advantages over large schools when implementing change, notably:

- The fact that the head is responsible for teaching a large proportion of the children means that s/he can implement curricular change directly;
- The limited size of staff means that few people need to be persuaded of the need for change and all can easily be involved (p. 32).

Taken together, these studies suggest that although heads of small primary schools may have no unique management tasks to perform, nevertheless their management and class-teaching tasks are generally affected by factors which in combination may be unique to small primary schools (Wallace 1988: 16–17). The job of headship in a small primary school seems to be distinctive in so far as the *context* in which management tasks have to be carried out is specific to small schools (p. 18). This context creates the organisational conditions whereby tensions exist between heads' teaching commitments and leading the school (Day *et al.* 2000 p. 162) and these tensions can often be acute and enduring.

While these are significant findings, they should not mask the fact that remarkably little work appears to have been conducted into *school leadership* in small primary schools. Furthermore, when this material is categorised into articles which are research-based and those which are commentary-oriented, the amount of empirical work into leadership in small primary schools can be seen as very meagre indeed. Clearly there is a lack of research into the role and work of heads, particularly in terms of leading school improvements and the systematic reporting of head teachers' perceptions and concerns.

If little has been written on the subject of leading small primary schools, the same is true with regard to leadership in large and very large schools. This group of schools appears to be the most under-researched of all. There is a dearth of material about them, despite statistics showing that they are increasing in number and cater for a growing proportion of primary-aged pupils. One study which has looked at larger schools is Wallace and Huckman's (1999) concerning senior management teams in primary schools. This research, conducted during the mid-1990s, looked at schools with over 300 pupils on roll and addressed the question: 'How do senior management teams (SMTs) in large primary sector schools operate where all members perceive themselves to be committed to teamwork as their core strategy for managing the school, and to what effect?' (Wallace and Huckman 1999: 28).

The research provides a detailed analysis and interpretation of senior management teams in four case-studied schools. The study suggests that SMTs have become a common component of management in most large schools (p. 191). The study also makes it plain that the key to effective SMTs rests upon the quality of teamwork. However, in drawing this conclusion the researchers also make it clear that there is a good deal of variation between management teams in different schools and that teamwork is complex and complicated by existing professional and organisational patterns, particularly hierarchical, role and accountability ones. For example, it is important that heads are willing to risk losing some control by sharing and delegating tasks (p. 202), even though they are ultimately accountable for the school. Thus while an elaborate hypothesis about SMTs is developed in the final chapter, Wallace and Huckman also say that:

> Arguments for the principle of sharing school management widely and equally may be persuasive in an ideal world, but they fail to take into account two features of the real world, at least in Britain: the possibility that sharing might result in ineffective management which is unacceptable because of the potential negative impact on pupils' education; and the strict hierarchy of accountability where the headteacher may have to answer for empowering colleagues if things go wrong.
>
> (p. 204)

While worthwhile, a team-based approach can be risky. Hence the researchers advise that heads use a 'contingency approach' based on school circumstances (pp. 204–5).

The shift to teamwork which the Wallace and Huckman study investigates is consistent with other trends in primary school management and organisation. Here I have in mind the move away from a teacher culture in primary schools concerned with professional independence towards one which today is much more concerned with professional interdependence (Southworth 2000). This movement has been accompanied, recently, by more collaborative approaches to management and leadership. However, it has been constrained by the accountability structures in our education system, which have supported the role assumptions of some head teachers who continue to retain all major decisions for themselves. This feature has been a long-standing theme in the study of primary-school leadership and management, being particularly evident in the literature on medium-sized schools.

Another study which included attention to school size and, in particular, referred to large primary schools, was that conducted into effective junior schools and departments in the Inner London Education Authority (ILEA) in the early 1980s. Mortimore *et al.*'s (1988) study suggested that in larger schools it was less common for heads to report that they asked teachers to provide regular forecasts of their teaching or to maintain individual records of children's progress. It was also found that:

> Such heads were less likely to have adopted a strategy of influencing teaching methods on a selective basis (only when judged 'necessary') and were more likely to have tried either to influence all teachers, or at the other extreme, to have made no attempt to exert any influence. They were also less likely to have influenced the curriculum of their school, or operated a school-based policy on in-service training. Moreover, in larger schools, staff were less likely to have been involved in the development of the school's guidelines than was the case in smaller schools.
>
> (Mortimore *et al.* 1988: 236)

Mortimore and his team do not specify the exact size of the schools included in their sample. They studied fifty, but only refer to the size of their year intakes. These ranged from sixteen children to 102, with thirty-six pupils being the average. They claim that their data showed support for middle- to small-sized schools with a junior roll of around 160 or fewer pupils. This range of size was linked positively to schools' effects on pupil progress, particularly in cognitive areas. Furthermore, there was 'no evidence from the Project's findings that larger schools were associated with better progress in any area' (p. 221).

Elsewhere they set out their thoughts about school size thus:

> The optimum size of schools is a much debated topic. Those who argue for large primary schools draw attention to the economy of scale, the richness of pooled resources, the availability of specialist staff, the existence of postholders with curriculum responsibilities and the availability of teaching support staff in the office, library and media resources areas of school life. Against these arguments the small school lobby can claim the benefit of greater teacher continuity, more detailed knowledge of pupils, closer co-operation and involvement with parents and the positive ethos that can only be captured in a small family setting. Interestingly, our data support neither view. As we noted in chapter 11, it was the schools with between one and two forms of entry which were more likely to be the most effective. Compared to village schools with just one or two teachers these are large, yet compared to primary schools with three or four forms of entry they are clearly small.
>
> (p. 274)

This is an interesting finding and one which they partially explain in terms of large schools finding it more difficult to maintain coherent, school-wide policies. Mortimore and his colleagues believed that through closer staff contact it may have been easier for heads of smaller schools to implement effective school-wide policies and to monitor the achievement of specific goals (p. 236).

These were interesting – even absorbing – findings. They raise a number of points. First, they focus on the benefits of smaller schools. In some ways this is an argument against large schools, but it includes doubts about small schools too. The emphasis is on smaller schools, not small schools. Given that the research was conducted in an urban setting, where there were many large schools, the study really suggests that medium-sized schools are the optimum size. Second, they highlight the importance of the number of forms of entry a school takes in rather than the overall size of the school, although there is an inevitable link between the two. Interestingly, in the study of large schools presented in Chapter 4, I found that it was when the number of forms of entry increased that this had a concomitant effect on school organisation. Third, the findings include a measure of speculation and thus cannot be taken at face value. There was clearly more to examine here.

My use of the past tense in the last sentence paves the way for a fourth and major point. Mortimore's research is now old and in many ways past its shelf life. It was conducted before we had a national curriculum, national assessments, literacy and numeracy strategies, school inspections and delegated financial management. Together these reforms have introduced ways of working which have addressed the shortcomings and weaknesses identified in the large schools criticised by Mortimore and his team. For example, school-wide policies are now common, as are teacher planning and the recording of pupils' progress. Thus the shortcomings identified by Mortimore above (p. 236) have probably been eliminated. Furthermore, monitoring on the part of head teachers has increased and changed from being an option to an obligation.

Indeed, the findings from the large schools research reported in Chapter 4, together with my ideas about learning-centred leadership given in Chapter 5, suggest that today heads are very much aware of the need to influence what happens in classrooms and work both directly and indirectly on this. Also, as this book develops, I will advance an argument in which learning-centred leadership is shown to take on different forms and emphases because of the effects of the school's size.

Nevertheless, the Mortimore study, despite being dated, raises some provocative ideas. Some of these ideas reappear in other places in this book, not least because heads continue to be sensitive to them. For example, heads of large schools were aware that size might negatively alter a school's ethos and that there could be a loss of 'family feel' in the school. Yet what also keeps resurfacing in the literature and discussions about school size is an argument restricted to that of little versus large schools. The debate has become polarised, with medium-sized schools being either taken for granted or overlooked. What the Mortimore study introduces is the benefit of a middle way and an argument for medium-sized schools. It is – as far as I have been able to detect – the only empirical study which takes this stance.

If there is a limited literature on leadership in small schools and very little on leadership in large schools, then it seems the literature on primary-school leadership is aimed at those in medium-sized schools. I suspect this conclusion is true. The general literature on primary-school leadership and management is characterised by a number of features. First, there has been a tendency for some of the writing to be prescriptive, with the publication of quite a number of 'how to do headship' – type texts. Second, an increasing number of descriptive studies and texts have appeared. These look at how heads use time, manage change and influence school cultures. Typically these studies and texts focus on aspects of head teachers' work, but to date only one has attempted a comprehensive account of a head teacher in action. This was my own study of a primary head at work over the course of a school year (Southworth 1995). Third, there has been a growing interest in leadership and school effectiveness, resulting in the view that the leadership qualities of head teachers and the manner in which they fulfil their management responsibilities are key factors in determining the effectiveness of their schools (Scottish Education Department 1990: 16).

Over time these studies have become increasingly analytical and have aided our understanding of the issues they focus on. Taken together, a number of common themes can be detected, and in a previous review of the literature (Southworth 1997) I identified six themes, three of which I will now highlight. First, I noted the lack of attention devoted to differences in school size. Indeed, the identification of this theme prompted me to begin a study – or rather a trilogy of studies – to examine similarities and differences in headship and school leadership in different-sized primary schools.

Second, the literature is dominated by research into head teachers. Remarkably little has been written on other leaders such as deputies and subject leaders. Thus the overall impression to be gained by the literature is that heads are important figures and others much less so. Since then some work has been published on deputies (Southworth 1998) and – as seen above – on senior management teams; but much more is needed. Head and deputy partnerships are now commonly spoken of, while the increase in SMTs and, possibly, leadership teams, suggests that there is much to be learned from looking at shared and distributed leadership in primary schools today.

Third, the texts themselves show heads to be powerful figures within 'their' schools: they are cast as pivotal, proprietorial and powerful individuals. Moreover, as noted above in Wallace and Huckman's study of primary schools' SMTs, responsibility and accountability structures tend to support these power relations in primary schools. This was certainly true of the head I observed in the close-up study I conducted in 1990 (Southworth 1995) and holds true for many heads with whom I have worked since.

These themes show that leadership in primary schools is strongly circumscribed by head teachers. For one reason: school leadership is viewed through the role and responsibilities of head teachers. Our preoccupation with heads means that we often, probably largely, perceive the roles of other teachers through the lens of the head. For another, the power and authority of heads governs what other leaders are able to do. A great deal rests on the dispositions of heads towards delegation and shared leadership.

However, as Wallace and Huckman emphasised, macro and micro contextual factors also impinge. The macro factors are the accountability structures present in the education system. The micro factors are the school-context ones, which include the school's performance levels, the quality of senior staff and experience of and attitudes towards shared leadership among senior and middle leaders.

Leading primary schools is thus a complex business. It revolves around head teachers but is also influenced by policy, system and school factors. It is contingent upon these factors as well upon the dispositions, attitudes and experience of individuals. Moreover, it is also influenced by school size, although it appears we know rather more about leading small primary schools than we do about leading very large ones, while the medium band of schools is both broad and numerous. All of which brings me back to the beginning: context matters, and size matters too. We need to look more closely and deeply at leadership in different-sized schools, as well as at other school features and the ways these impinge on schools, in order to gain a more discriminating and mature understanding of the nature and character of leadership in different schools. Hence the next three chapters focus in turn on leadership in small, medium-sized and large schools.

Part 2

Leading small, medium-sized and large schools

2 Leading small primary schools

This chapter reports on the findings of the research I conducted into successful head teachers in small-sized primary schools. The full report of the research is much longer than this single chapter, so what appears here is a reduced version and omits some aspects of the research which are not relevant to the focus of this book. The chapter is divided into four parts. In the first part I briefly set out the aims, purposes and methods of the study. In the second I present what the chosen head teachers said about their work, along with what some of their teachers and governors also said. In the third I will discuss my reflections and insights into headship in small primary schools, while in the fourth I will present my conclusions.

Aims and methods

This research investigated a sample of successful head teachers in small sized primary schools focusing on their approaches to leadership and school improvement. The research was funded by the Teacher Training Agency, with additional support being provided by the University of Reading School of Education. The research aimed to:

- Explore how the studied head teachers led their schools' improvement efforts;
- Identify from their testimonies the characteristics and strategies they associated with effective school leadership;
- Discover how these heads were professionally prepared for headship and developed their leadership skills over time.

I embarked on the study for three reasons. Firstly, as noted in the previous chapter, there is a need to develop a more differentiated view of primary school leadership. Secondly, such studies as have been conducted into primary headship are ageing because of recent reforms in education and there is a need to update our knowledge and understanding of leaders' roles. Thirdly, while it is widely recognised that school leadership matters, we still need to know more about successful heads and other leaders and how they improve and transform their schools. Moreover, this viewpoint is one that is central to the role of research at the National College for School Leadership.

The study focused on a sample of ten primary heads working in small schools. After considerable thought I decided to study schools with fewer than 150 pupils on roll rather than restrict my sample to those with fewer than a hundred pupils, the more usual threshold for defining small schools in the United Kingdom. I chose the higher limit because I wanted to look at schools with less than one-form entry, since I thought there might be value in looking at them. I also adopted a lower limit and chose not to study schools with fewer than fifty pupils on roll. I aimed for the sample to include, as far as possible, heads from rural, suburban and urban settings, denominational and non-denominational schools and schools from a number of LEAs.

Schools were chosen from the Beacons of Excellence list and LEA nominations, which were then checked against what the schools' OFSTED inspection reports said about each school, its setting and its head's leadership before drawing up a 'shortlist' of prospective participants. All who were contacted agreed to participate.

Fieldwork involved one day spent visiting each of the chosen schools and inter-viewing the heads, two teachers and one governor. I included staff and governors in order to develop a more rounded view of their roles. Such an approach has begun to take root in recent years (e.g. Day *et al.* 2000) and has the benefit of showing us something about 'how well heads' practices conform to teachers' mental models of what leaders do: their leader prototypes' as Leithwood argues in his foreword to Day *et al.* (2000: xiii). On the day of the visit an initial tour of the school was made with the head enabling them to highlight any context-specific issues they might wish to be noted and allowing me to familiarise myself with the school as a setting for their leadership. The tour was followed by interviews first with the head and then with the other three individuals. Towards the end of my time in the school I met with the head again to see if they had anything further to add or to follow up lines of enquiry which had emerged during the day.

Findings from the head teacher, teacher and governor interviews

The initial tours of the schools and their sites showed in what ways each school differed from the others. One was located in an isolated rural area; another was an historic building. One was surrounded by high-rise dwellings and close to a major motorway. Some of the schools had plenty of space, including attractive halls for PE, while others were cramped, with space at a premium. In some all the teaching was conducted in the main building; in others, temporary class-rooms had been added to the original construction.

Head-teacher data and findings

As the heads showed me around their schools they demonstrated their concern for the quality of the buildings and site. They talked about the condition of the fabric of the school and pointed out developments either accomplished or planned. I saw new entrance areas, halls and classrooms, extensions and recently added staffrooms. While all these things mattered to the heads, first and foremost their attention to the physical state of the school revealed their desire to ensure that the pupils worked in the best possible learning environment.

At the same time, the heads also made it plain that they were keenly aware of the school as a setting for their headship and leadership. Each told me about their school's past and how it had come to be what it was. Each described in some detail what the school had been like when they started their period of headship. They all implicitly demonstrated that their priorities and actions were contingent upon the school's past and present circumstances.

As I was shown around I was introduced to every member of staff, and I was expected to greet all the teaching and classroom support staff, site agents and caretakers, office staff and parents and governors working in the school on that day. All the heads showed their awareness of colleagues and supporters. Everyone was noticed, recognised and valued. Interpersonal relationships formed a major feature of their work and they conducted these with a firm, transparent sense of care and consideration for others.

While the tours revealed some aspects of the heads' leadership, the interviews highlighted many others. In the following subsections I shall present what they said about: becoming a head teacher; what headship was like; their own professional development; leading school improvement; and school leadership.

Becoming a head teacher

Asked why they had become heads, a number of reasons were given. While they had all been deputy heads (although one had only been a deputy for two months before becoming acting head), five had found that role a less than satisfying one:

> *I was frustrated as a deputy – I did not quite know who I was as a deputy.*

> *I enjoyed deputy headship at first and then I became frustrated.*

Only two had had positive experiences as deputies, but these had recognised after a period in post that they needed to move on. Most acknowledged that they wanted the responsibility headship was perceived to offer:

> *I was immensely curious about headship, about being a head . . . So eventually I decided to be a head teacher. Some of headship is having the power to do what you think is right and proper.*

> *I felt I could make a difference and wanted to try (headship).*

These heads saw headship as a position which would enable them to make a major contribution to the school. They wanted to see for themselves whether they could meet the challenge of being a school leader and also implement their educational beliefs. For these reasons the role appears to be both an empowerment and a personal challenge.

It is empowering because these individuals had reached the position where they had the authority and power to determine what their schools should be like and the direction in which they ought to be heading. For at least half these heads this was, compared to deputy headship, 'liberating'. They were free from the constraints of dealing with their former superiors' wishes and (relatively) free to work towards their educational values and priorities. Hence, the role appears in some respects relates to achieving a sense of self-actualisation.

At the same time, the role is a challenge because the responsibility is now theirs and they have to prove to the schools' stakeholders that they really can make a difference. They also have to prove to themselves that they really can make a difference, and put into practice what they believe in and make these ideals work.

What is headship like?

The first thing the heads mentioned was that headship was hard work:

> It is hard work. That is not a gripe, but a fact. I do not dislike hard work – it is extremely time-consuming and it is very mind-consuming. I find my mind drifts to work. I spend a lot of time rehearsing ideas.

On occasion they found the role very tiring. A number of reasons were offered for the tiring nature of the work, including dealing with so many people and the variety of the tasks they attended to, but mostly it revolved around the dual demands of head and teacher, as one said: *It is exhausting teaching and head teachering.*

Although the double load of leading and teaching is bound to be challenging, and energy levels are inevitably going to be depleted towards the end of each term, this double load is accompanied by other 'drivers' which propelled these heads. Their reasons for wanting to become heads suggest they were highly motivated and driven by their own personal needs to meet their own goals, to their own standards. They had high expectations of themselves. It seems that these ten shared similarities with the six heads in Hayes' (1996) study reviewed in Chapter 1. They all aimed to achieve high standards in every area of the job. Yet this goal sometimes leads to exhaustion because heads work so hard to achieve it and also to conceal their shortcomings. Therefore headship may be demanding for three related reasons:

- Heads of small schools are 'doubly loaded' being both heads and have teaching duties to perform, which for some were very substantial class teaching responsibilities;
- They have to meet the expectations of all those they serve and lead;
- They have to match up to their own expectations and ambitions.

In other words, the double load is really a triple one. They are coping with two roles and their own internal expectations and standards.

The most satisfying features of headship were:

Seeing children's progress and also seeing the staff's satisfaction.

The best bits are going into classrooms, sharing the children's successes.

I enjoy final responsibility – which is where the challenge is for me. Whenever I want to maintain perspective, I go into the classes.

Making the school run like I want a school to run and watching everything come together: school, village, parents, and staff.

The worst features of headship were:

The long hours and continuous nature of headship – there is a never-endingness to headship. There used to be a time when there were 'busy periods' during the year, but now it is all year long.

The constant paperwork – you really do have to swim the channel every day. Plus the expectation of everyone that as head you'll have an answer.

Not enough time, not enough money and the external agenda. Dealing with someone else's agenda is difficult.

Much that is stated here was repeated later in the interviews when I asked the heads to characterise headship. Each offered a few keywords which, when put together, form three categories: positive; negative; and graphic, by which I mean words or phrases they used to describe some aspect of headship or to portray what the role felt like to them.

The positive terms used were: 'exciting', 'exhilarating', 'wonderful', 'inspiring', 'rewarding', 'fulfilling'. The negative ones were: 'extremely hard work', 'demanding', 'exhausting', 'tiring', 'too much'. The graphic descriptions included these observations:

Diverse – rich, varied, fragmented.

Juggling time, money, and loyalties – between home and school.

You are in the middle of things – at the heart of things – there is an immediacy about it.

These comments are consistent with what other primary heads have said in recent times. The 'juggling' metaphor and that of the plate spinner, remain the most popular images of headship, although it seems that the number of plates heads have to keep spinning has increased in recent years, while heads of small schools may be seen as having to keep both the school plates and their own classroom plates spinning simultaneously.

Professional development

Asked how they had developed as head teachers, most felt that over time they had grown in confidence. Some had benefited from mentors during the early years of headship, although others had not found this very helpful, largely because they had not been well matched to their mentors. Five spoke of the value of belonging to local head-teacher support groups or clusters:

> *I'm in a small cluster group of four heads. We have worked together on assessment and we get together twice a term. It's a good antidote to loneliness. We phone each other too.*

While all the heads had one or more colleagues they could turn to for advice or use as 'sounding boards', they also acknowledged that most of their professional and role-learning was done on the job:

> *Most of my learning has been doing the job, living it. Meeting problems and working through them.*

The majority did not regard deputy headship as a valuable preparation for headship. Of the two who did, one had been a deputy in two schools and had worked with four heads.

Other forms of professional development the heads considered significant for them were advanced diplomas, an in-service B.Ed. course, Open University courses and some deputy-head management courses run by universities or their local authorities. LEA advisory support was also valued by many of them.

Looking to the future, the heads anticipated they would benefit from particular learning opportunities. Most frequently mentioned was the need to keep up to date with developments in ICT. Three wanted to enhance their knowledge and understanding of monitoring, evaluation and target-setting. Two were considering doing something academic, such as a master's degree, because they wanted to 'see a wider picture' and 'look at something in depth'.

Most obvious from what the heads said about their experience of professional development was their implicit belief in self-development. They saw themselves as developing and valued professional learning. Many praised off-site courses and in-service programmes, but on the whole their development as head teachers had come about through experiential learning. What characterised their growth as school leaders most of all was how much they had learned from actually doing the job, meeting the challenges thrown up by their work and dealing with whatever they encountered. Perhaps, then, it is not surprising that for at least half these heads one of the most significant developments that had occurred was the growth in their confidence and sense of self. The sense of finding your own way and dealing with whatever happens possibly highlights the major tests of headship, at least in the early years, if not the ensuing ones. Their comments also relate to having to prove to themselves that they really can make a difference. The ability to cope and survive the trials and challenges of being a leader develops one's self-esteem and self-image as a head teacher. This creates role credibility, both in relation to their work colleagues and in their own estimation.

School improvement

All the heads believed their schools to be improving. When asked to say in what ways they saw them as improving, they replied at length, drawing on a range of indicators. The following extracts represent their comments:

> *Academically we are improving. The children haven't changed, what they are capable of hasn't changed, but what they produce has altered. Results are getting better, but it has taken time. Improvement is a long job. The teaching is now better, there are no holes in the teaching or the curriculum as there were. The* minimum *levels we provide for all children are so much higher – we offer solid, consistent programmes of work. We have developed long, medium and short-term planning and ended up looking at what good teaching is and what good learning looks like. We developed a policy about 'Children learn best when . . .'*

> *Standards are improving. Pupil attitudes are much better. The children are much happier. Behaviour is far better, especially in the playground. Our SATs scores have gone up.*

> *There is zero tolerance of failure here. We really do want every child to succeed and all to achieve their full potential. We work on attitudes, on behaviour and motivation. Our SATs results are very high. We unpick the scores very carefully because in a high-scoring school, improvement is harder. We are an analytical staff. I look at the scores, for example, there were not enough level 3s at the end of KS 1 last year. It looks to be so much better this year. Teacher consistency is also very important. Tenacity is so important in improvement.*

In leading the schools' improvement efforts the heads employed a range of strategies. Some spoke directly about using their teaching as an example:

> *Throughout I have drawn heavily on my teaching and that has been hugely important with the staff. They know I have done in my teaching what they are being asked to do.*

Another strategy common to all the heads was monitoring. This took a number of forms, including formal and informal approaches, head-teacher and peer observation of classrooms, examining pupils' work and scrutinising teacher plans:

> *It is important to really know the children and to know what is going on in the classrooms. I call that quality control. Monitoring by me, the deputy and the coordinators is essential.*

> *We make sure we are clear about what we are looking for before we monitor and then, as a staff, discuss what we find. Monitoring helps us to set high teacher expectations and to sustain existing ones. Statistics and value-added are also important and evidence and analysis are really important today. Constant evaluation is so important.*

The heads used a great deal of staff discussion to move the schools along. At many points in the interviews it was clear they valued professional dialogue. Discussions were viewed as useful ways of raising teacher expectations, challenging assumptions, developing a greater consistency of approach and establishing and sustaining a common vision for improvements in teaching and learning.

Yet while professional talk was understood as a means of improving the school, it was not seen as sufficient. These heads had also devoted a lot of time and effort to creating and developing a series of organisational and curricular structures and systems to support improvement efforts and to ensure quality in teaching and learning. These included:

- School improvement planning
- Target-setting
- Analyses of pupil learning data
- Evaluation of pupil, cohort, key stage and school performance levels
- Policies for learning and teaching
- Curriculum policies
- Assessment and marking policies
- Monitoring
- Weekly planning by teachers using learning objectives
- Staff meetings
- Subject leaders' roles.

As well as asking the heads to talk about how their schools were improving and how they were leading these efforts, I invited them to talk more specifically about two aspects of school improvement. The first was how they influenced what went on in classrooms, and the second was whether and how they focused on the quality of teaching.

In terms of influencing classrooms, a number of tactics were used. The formulation and implementation of policies was one, the policies being concerned with the curriculum, teaching and learning. Five spoke of teachers' plans in terms of the learning objectives teachers were setting and of teachers planning together to develop consistent approaches across the classes and to share expertise. Four heads also mentioned the analysis of pupil learning data and outcomes. The use of personal example was mentioned as well:

> *It is a question of example. I will teach anywhere. Staff understand that, they also know I monitor – I'll visit their classes and pick up a tray of pupils' books and look at them. I hope a lot of my influence is through example, when I teach, when I lead the sharing assemblies on Fridays.*

The most common approach, however, was through discussion:

> *Mostly I influence what is going on in classrooms through professional discussion. We talk about our practice.*

Some of the heads also raised issues with colleagues, seeded ideas in the minds of others, or asked questions:

> *I feed into staff awareness certain questions or issues and question pupils' progress and outcomes. A lot comes from asking pertinent questions such as: 'If we think we are good at, how come . . . ?' Or 'We do this really well, how can we use this to make X better?'*

The heads' responses to the question about whether and how they focused on teaching overlapped with much of the foregoing. Some were monitoring the quality of teaching and teachers' plans, as implied in previous statements. In three schools the formulation, implementation and development of a whole-school policy for teaching and learning was regarded as having a significant impact on teaching. Some had followed up OFSTED inspectors' comments about teaching; others had used the literacy and numeracy strategies to highlight issues about pedagogy. Three of the heads had in previous times been obliged to be direct with certain colleagues (who had now left the schools) about poor or weak teaching.

However, most of them sought to accentuate the positive and reinforce good practice, which they did through discussion. As before, professional discussion and dialogue were highly valued ways of influencing practice:

> *We talk professionally about where we can improve, not where someone is doing something wrong.*

A number of ideas emerge from these heads' comments about school improvement. All saw themselves as leading players and regarded this issue as *the* main part of their role. They all understood headship to be about developing the quality of the pupils' learning and enhancing pupils' progress.

No head relied on a single approach to school improvement; rather they each employed a variety of strategies to influence the practice of teachers and classroom support staff. Generally they monitored what was happening in the classrooms and across the school. They were most interested in what the children and teachers were actually doing and in whether they were doing what they said or thought they were. They were keen to concentrate on what was happening inside classrooms and the received curriculum as well as the planned curriculum and the taught curriculum. Monitoring included: classroom observation; looking at teachers' plans, learning objectives and thus teacher expectations; curricula coverage, both in terms of breadth and balance; looking at pupils' work; looking at pupil outcome and progress data. In other words, all the heads were – more or less – using an evidence-based approach to improvement.

They had also put in place a range of other structures and systems to support school improvement. School development plans were evident in all the schools; in some they were very prominent, displayed on staffroom walls or in the head teachers' offices. School policies for curriculum subjects, SEN and assessment were frequently cited as steering the direction of practice across the school. Most telling, however, seemed to be the introduction and adoption of policies for teaching and/or learning. These took on a central importance in some of the schools. Some of these heads had used them as the foundation for improving their schools, while others had made them their touchstone for evaluating quality.

Integral to policy development and planning processes were staff discussions. Sustaining teacher talk and using this as a vehicle for teacher and staff development underscored almost everything these heads were doing. Talk enabled shared understandings to be developed, levels of awareness and expectations to be raised and common approaches to become established. The heads presented themselves as adroit at questioning assumptions and skilful in probing any complacency they encountered.

Wherever possible the heads were keen to involve colleagues and develop the leadership roles of others. Where a school had a deputy head, that individual was seen as a partner. Subject leaders figured prominently too. Teamwork was something all the heads mentioned at some point in their interviews. All were keenly aware of the importance of staff working closely together, of them becoming a cooperative group in which individuals supported one another and acted as a combined teaching unit. All saw the success of the school as resting upon the participation of the entire staff. The heads valued professional collaboration and a particular kind of staff culture; this also relates to the next section, since one characteristic of their leadership was teamwork.

Leadership

When the heads were asked what lessons they had learned about school leadership, three sets of ideas were identified. The first – and overwhelmingly the most important set in terms of the number of times the heads mentioned it – was working with others, teamwork and sharing leadership. The second was the need for heads to be forward-looking. The third was being knowledgeable and leading by example.

Working with others was mentioned by nine of the heads:

> *You have to find a way of getting everyone on your side. You need to like people. Things will evolve over time so long as you do not de-motivate people.*

> *You have to know how to manage staff and to value and appreciate people and be there for the staff.*

> *The greatest thing is to build up a school and that is a team effort.*

Comments about shared leadership included one head saying they thought it was inappropriate for leadership to be invested in one person: 'I don't want the school to be me.' Others stressed the importance of delegation and the need to recognise that everyone was a leader.

The second group of points covered the idea that leaders need to be forward-looking and visionary:

> *Leadership is to do with looking ahead, seeing where you want to be.*

> *You have got to know where you want to go – vision.*

One emphasised the importance of focusing on what could be achieved:

> *You have got to think about the possibilities and not the limitations. In a small school there are limitations – often financial – but you have to think your way around them, otherwise you'll get stuck.*

The third group of points concentrated on knowledge, particularly professional knowledge, since the heads knew that this gave you credibility with the staff, governors and parents and enabled you to lead by example:

> *You need the knowledge of teaching and learning and the curriculum to lead teachers.*

> *You have to keep your finger on the pulse – know what is going on in classrooms.*

> *You have to lead by example.*

When I asked what they saw as their strengths, some of the same points were mentioned, but, interestingly, others were raised as well. They are presented as a simple list in order for readers to compare and contrast with the foregoing insights. Where they were stated more than once, the figure in brackets indicates the frequency.

- Listener (5)
- Hard-working (4)
- Try not to be ruffled; stay calm (2)
- Communicate clearly (2)
- Patient with adults (2)
- Appreciative of staff (2)
- Consider the children's needs in everything I do (2)
- Fight for resources (2)
- Stamina and perseverance
- Commitment to others
- Organised
- Reliable

- Practical
- Enjoy talking – but listening is important.
- I never knowingly ask someone to do something I wouldn't do.
- Not confrontational
- Forward thinker
- Sense of humour
- Enthusiastic
- Can stand my ground.

These points show that the heads regarded school leadership as requiring them to be enthusiastic, positive and determined. Yet because they were working with colleagues and regarded teamwork as vital to the school's success they were alert to staff needs. They therefore recognised that leaders must be sensitive to others, valuing and involving them as well as encouraging them to take a lead.

What also begins to emerge is a range of images about leadership. At different points and times the heads portrayed leadership as being concerned with maintenance, as interpersonal, and concerned with both change and survival. The maintenance image relates to the heads' comments about being organised, using time wisely and establishing common practices, systems and structures in the school. They clearly appreciated that things had to be well managed. They were also aware that leadership was relational because it was about working with people. The notion of creating and sustaining productive professional relations within a small group of staff working alongside one another in close proximity was uppermost in their minds. Yet, while positive relations had to be sustained, staff also needed to change and hone their practices. The 'change' image lies at the heart of leading school improvements. The 'survival' image stems from the fact that headship is hard work. Words such as 'determination', 'strength', 'struggle', 'fight' and 'battle' were used by several respondents, particularly the newer heads, and/or those working in schools that had been performing poorly. There was a general recognition that you sometimes had to be tenacious as well as direct and frank with colleagues. Moreover, given that these schools did not have lavish amounts of funding, many of the heads had fought for additional resources. All this strength and effort nevertheless took its toll on them, and all at some stage acknowledged that they had become fatigued and needed to pace themselves. Thus the survival image relates to institutional and individual aspects of their work. It is about the school struggling through to success and the heads coping on a personal level, meeting the many and varied challenges they encountered day by day.

Leadership itself is largely understood as meaning six things. Firstly, it is about looking forward: leaders provide the school with a sense of direction. Secondly, leaders deal with and manage change. They are – as the previous section showed – school improvers. They see themselves and their schools as moving forward, recognise that this process has to be led and managed and want the children to achieve as much as they possibly can. Thirdly, the process of leading rests on the power of example. The idea of leading by professional example, either as a class teacher drawing on their knowledge of the curriculum and children, or through their attitudes to change, improvement and leadership, lies at the heart of their work. Fourthly, leadership was understood as interpersonal, as about working with others – which could be fun, frustrating, challenging and rewarding. Fifthly, they were aware that their leadership had to suit the circumstances they faced at any one time. Sixthly, the heads were most strongly anchored by their responsibilities for the pupils. At the very heart of what they said lay an unrelenting concern for the children and their progress.

These ideas show that leadership, for these head teachers, is neither one-dimensional nor monochrome. It calls for many qualities and skills, and no single style was favoured by the heads or thought to be appropriate for all.

Teacher data and findings

Two general observations must be made at the outset about the teacher interviews. Firstly, all were positive about their head teachers as school leaders. No one dissented from the view that their heads were successful. Some were a little more muted than others, while many – indeed most – were very positive about them. Secondly, the leadership characteristics the teachers noted about them are broadly in line with those discussed by the heads in the previous section.

Asked what the heads had achieved in their schools, the teachers' responses showed they believed these individuals had had a positive impact there. Some talked about how their schools' pupil numbers were either rising or had risen since the time of their heads' taking up their appointments. Others described how the school had been transformed:

> *There has been a complete turnaround in the attitude of the children.*

> *She has raised standards.*

> *Academic standards are now very high.*

> *We had a fantastic OFSTED. She said it was down to us, but we had the leadership at the top.*

Others talked about how the heads had improved the school sites, resources and buildings:

> *She is good at pushing for site improvements – the playground, buildings, new classrooms, a conservation area, and she has established the nursery.*

> *The physical look of the school has improved, classrooms have been gutted, stuff cleared away, lots of redecoration, carpeting, and displays.*

The teachers noted that the heads had influenced the quality of staff relations and pupil behaviour, increased teacher expectations, revised curriculum planning, introduced curricular policies and schemes, enhanced relations with parents and the wider community and modernised the school as a whole. Taken together, these constitute an impressive endorsement of the heads' achievements.

Given such faith in the heads' efforts, I explored why the teachers thought these individuals were so successful. Approximately fourteen different reasons were offered by the respondents, many of which were cited by more than one teacher. They are listed here with the frequencies given in parentheses:

- Hard-working (10)
- Enables collaborative working (7)
- Leads by example (4)
- Approachable (3)
- Determined (3)
- Visionary (3)
- Praises staff (3)
- Knows what is going on (3)
- Good listener (3)
- Sets high expectations (2)
- Fair
- Dedicated
- Organised
- Good relationships with children.

Much was said about how hard their heads worked, about teamwork and leading by example:

> She puts huge amounts of time, effort and energy into it. She has given this place everything. Her commitment, dedication and her energy is . . . oh . . . enormous. She just keeps going.

> He puts in an incredible amount of time, he works incredibly hard.

> There is a good feel of teamwork. She is the leader, but she is a good team player.

> Everyone is made to feel they play a part in making the school successful.

> She leads by example, she is not just a manager, she will teach and she knows where you are coming from. She understands teaching and she is not removed from the classroom.

> She leads by example, which I find really motivating.

Asked later in the interviews to characterise their heads' leadership, they mentioned many of the same qualities and skills. The most popular characteristics were:

- Approachable (8)
- Hard-working (7)
- Leads by example (4)
- Has clear ideas/vision (4).

Asked to reflect on whether and how their heads had influenced their work as teachers, they made comments which implied that three related strategies had shaped their own thinking and practice. The first was the heads' monitoring and knowledge of what was happening around their schools and inside classrooms. The second concerned the heads' teaching methods, behaviour and attitudes towards the children, which were seen as models of good practice. The third were the opportunities allowed for discussion with colleagues, including the head, which developed ideas and teaching knowledge.

Governor data and findings

Ten school governors were interviewed, one in each school. Seven were chairs of governors, one a vice-chair, one the special educational needs governor and one a governor with no additional responsibilities.

Asked to describe the heads' achievements, these governors spoke on several aspects of their schools' development. The following extracts speak more directly and clearly about the heads' work than any summary statement I could draft:

> *She has achieved a phenomenal amount. My child was not going to go to this school, but the head encouraged me to have another look and when I did, I changed my mind because I was inspired by her teaching. She has built up pupils' self-esteem [and] developed trust in the school.*

> *He has pulled the school together well. It is a very popular school with parents. Achieved a lot with the buildings – the school hall is excellent thanks to him. The parents are much more involved now. It's the general atmosphere – the friendly, co-operative staff. He has built a team and brought people together.*

> *She has steered the school through to becoming a modern, successful primary school. The school was in a mess when she became head. Primary schools depend hugely on their heads. Heads give the flavour to the school. We have a highly motivated and qualified staff . . . The school has grown and new buildings have been added. She has hauled up the standards hugely.*

Clearly the governors believed their heads to be doing a good job. They spoke warmly and positively of them throughout the interviews; they appreciated their efforts and achievements. While the general tenor of their comments is consistent with what the teachers said, the governors laid greater stress on two aspects of the heads' work than did the teachers. First, they were very much aware of how the heads had raised or sustained the schools' reputations and standing with the parents. Second, it was noted by several governors how well the heads worked with them. Therefore, while acknowledging how these heads had improved or transformed the schools in ways consistent with what the heads and teachers said, the governors were aware that external relations and – in particular, dealings with parents – were important elements in running a successful school.

When asked why they thought the heads were successful leaders, the governors emphasised that it was because they never lost sight of the children. They also saw the heads' capacity to work hard as an important factor. More than the teachers, the governors were aware of the administrative load head teachers had to deal with: the volume of paperwork – forms, documentation, finances, and letters – was mentioned by several. Others stressed how well organised the heads were and praised their efficiency. They described their heads as approachable and calm in their dealings with colleagues, parents and the governors themselves.

Asked to characterise the heads' leadership, two noted the heads' knowledge of the curriculum and of wider educational issues. The heads' organisational skills were mentioned on three occasions, as were their approachability and their capacity to involve others. Valuing everyone was highlighted twice, as were leading by example, being a good teacher and working hard. Items mentioned just once included: enthusiasm, encouragement, being strong, attention to detail, imagination and delegating to others.

When attempting to summarise the heads' approaches to leadership, the governors quite spontaneously provided thumbnail sketches. For example:

> *She has a huge love of children. Delights in providing pupils with resources and experiences, such as computers, visits and books. Excited by each child's step along the learning pathway. Hugely dedicated. Courageous – had to fight for things.*

> *He likes to think it is not him but the group; but it isn't, it's him.*

> *She's a workaholic – her heart and soul is school, school and school.*

> *She is in charge. She knows what she wants and she achieves. She positively enjoys teaching.*

> *He leads by example, in everything.*

These portraits add to the developing picture of headship. When seen alongside the characteristics the governors identified in answering the previous question, these sketches suggest that headship is not about a single 'style' but has more to do with employing a repertoire of skills and qualities. Given that these heads did make use of a range of strategies, what the governors' summary descriptions imply is that within the broader repertoire of skills, individuals emphasised or favoured certain combinations.

Asked to comment whether and how the heads influenced the work of teachers, the governors' replies support the threefold typology advanced from the analysis of the teachers' comments. Monitoring, modelling and professional discussion were the main ways in which the governors saw the heads as influencing practice.

Discussion and reflections

Eight interrelated themes emerge from these findings, which I shall now discuss in turn.

Working hard

It is clear from the testimonies of the heads, teachers and governors that being a head teacher is hard work: respondents from all three groups repeatedly made this point. The heads acknowledged that they worked hard, but did so in an uncomplaining way. They appeared to regard this as a fact of headship rather than something they might be able to avoid or change. Moreover, it was clear that these ten individuals had an appetite for hard work. They plainly enjoyed the responsibilities of headship. Indeed, it is probable that one of the reasons why they were comfortable with the demands of their role was that having made the conscious decision to become head teachers they were still proving to themselves either that they could do the job successfully or that they could sustain their success.

More than this, though, it also seems that hard work is necessary if heads are to be successful. For one thing, in small schools – which by definition have fewer staff – heads do not have many colleagues they can turn to. As more than one said, heads in small schools have to 'muck in'. They had no personal assistants nor many – or any – of the trappings of executive life in commerce and industry. Instead, each school employed a 'secretary' who managed most aspects of school administration and finance, and what was not done by them was left for the heads to do.

The other reason why hard work is necessary centres on what the teachers and governors said. It was clear from the respondents' comments that in recognising the amount of time and effort the heads put into their role they were acknowledging not only the fact that these individuals had a capacity for hard work but also that they were strongly committed to their schools. Dealing with all the demands and not shrinking from all the requirements of the role were indicators – indeed, symbols – of the heads' concern and dedication. Hard work is thus not simply about being prepared to put in the hours and get through the tasks; it is also a powerful emblem of that person's devotion to the school.

Determination

Undoubtedly the heads were resolute about their schools doing well and working tenaciously towards increased levels of success, as the discussion about school improvement below demonstrates. Here, though, I want to highlight how they showed determination concerning a number of other aspects of the school.

As each head showed me round their school site and buildings it was obvious that they had striven to develop the quality of the school as a learning environment for the children. Their efforts were noted by the governors and teachers. Sometimes their ability to secure additional resources was seen as a sign of their commitment to the school. Without a doubt, the governors and teachers recognised that their heads were 'fighters'. For example, several had battled for new or better buildings. Sometimes they had persisted in the face – initially, at least – of a lack of concern from other agencies. On such occasions the governors had acknowledged the heads' perseverance and courage.

It also seems that these fighting qualities stem not so much from a desire to win as from wanting the very best for the children. On many occasions the heads showed they were not prepared to put up with what they regarded as second-best teaching or poor learning conditions, resources or equipment. Hence they had found ways of improving the schools' physical and material environments. In so doing they demonstrated not only determination but also entrepreneurial skills because they had enhanced the school by tapping into different sources of funding and making successful bids for monies.

Positive

All these heads shared one characteristic: they were strongly positive individuals, as was shown particularly through their beliefs about the school, its staff and its pupils. They all believed their schools would improve and become increasingly successful. They were quick to acknowledge their schools' past and present successes, often describing these as resulting from the children's or the staff's efforts.

They were also very optimistic. They knew they had challenges to face and resolve, but more than anything they viewed the future with hope. There was no sense of despondency or discontent – even though some were stern critics of certain initiatives – while several considered small schools to be undervalued and overlooked. In addition to being welcoming to me and others, they were enthusiastic about their schools and about the future.

Approachable

The heads' ability to make me feel welcome was not something specially put on for my benefit. The majority of teachers commented on the fact that their heads were approachable. Some governors also reported that the heads were accessible to them, their staff, parents and members of the local community.

It also seems that staff in particular respond positively to heads who are accessible. The frequency with which this attribute was mentioned suggests that teachers approve of heads who are not remote, are willing to talk and listen to them and share their ideas and plans with staff. Therefore the notion of the heads being approachable persons is probably a form of shorthand for their being expected to be communicative and receptive leaders who acknowledge others and interact well with them on a personal and professional level. Certainly there is a great deal of corroborative evidence that all the heads worked along these lines and that this approach found favour with teachers and governors. Furthermore, such an approach also relates to the next point.

Team-builders and players

Running through all the data sets is a common theme about teamwork. This emphasis is no surprise given that in recent times teacher collaboration has become a norm in primary schools, as evidenced by attention to collaborative staff cultures and 'whole school' policymaking (Nias *et al.* 1989, 1992). However, in small primary schools the emphasis may be particularly important. Many respondents appeared aware that if the school was to be successful then its staff had to work together. Ensuring that the school was a cohesive organisation, that the staff cooperated with one another, that communications worked well and the staff shared ideas, resources and supported one another are now common expectations of heads.

Part of teamwork was developing shared leadership at all levels, although this was not always achieved because staff groups were very small and some members were seen as not yet ready for taking a lead. The teachers, too, saw benefits from participating and acknowledged how effective their heads were in orchestrating staff collaboration. More than anything, though, the heads' awareness that positive inter-professional relations were critical to the health of the school, and that dealing with staff, parents and others was the key skill area of leadership – something teachers and governors also acknowledged – supports this claim that teamwork was a central theme. In other words, both staff and governors appreciated that in small schools everyone had to be involved and play their part.

If teamwork is essential, then the heads' contribution to it followed two paths. First, the heads were team *builders*. Second, they were team *players*. They all demonstrated that they had been active in creating teams in their respective schools. They recognised and valued individuals and encouraged participation in planning, policymaking and school decisions. The emphasis they placed on staff discussion and professional dialogue was another hallmark of their concern to develop and sustain collaboration. They also, however, valued the staff as a group: they were quick to attribute success to the group's efforts rather than to their own. In this way they suggested they were also team players: success was not 'mine' but 'ours'. This was not false modesty but a genuine appreciation of collaborative effort and achievement. The heads knew that while they played a leading part in their schools they could achieve little single-handedly and that whatever success their schools had achieved was the result of a combined effort on the part of everyone.

Teamwork applied to all staff members, including office and classroom support colleagues; but more than anything, improving the performance of the school depended on the teaching staff functioning as a combined teaching unit. In these schools, developing a team of teachers characterised by professional openness, unity of purpose, shared goals and educational values, consistency in teaching and planning, continuity in the curriculum and agreed and implemented classroom practices was both the means and end of teamwork.

School improvers

All these heads were improving their schools. For some it was because they had been appointed to move the schools forward; for others it was more a case of enhancing already high levels of success. Whatever the context, none were satisfied for things to remain as they were. Thus they spoke about wanting to avoid complacency within the school, of pupil results rising, of underachievement being eliminated, of pupils' rates of progress accelerating, of children's attitudes to learning becoming more positive and of the schools' ethos changing for the better. All the heads wanted to improve on their previous best and to establish and sustain norms of continuous improvement in their schools.

Each used a number of strategies to improve the quality of teaching and learning in the school, but three broad strategies stand out from what all the respondents said:

- Modelling
- Monitoring
- Professional dialogue and discussion.

Each of these called for a range of tactics. For example, modelling involved the heads using their teaching as an example of what and how to do things, working alongside staff in their classrooms, coaching staff through demonstrating how they themselves taught topics or approached issues and making conscious use of assemblies as occasions for promoting and reinforcing educational values and practice.

Monitoring involved the heads looking at teachers' weekly plans and the learning objectives they were working towards, visiting classrooms, examining samples of pupils' work, using coordinators to observe implementation of curricula policies and teaching and learning, reviewing pupil test and assessment information and evaluating pupil, class and school levels of performance and progress.

Professional dialogue was developed through staff meetings, the process of putting together curricular policies, reviewing practice, looking at pupil learning data, joint planning meetings and general teamwork. The heads also followed up visits to classrooms with informal discussions with individuals, or used questions to probe teachers' assumptions and to promote ideas and ways forward.

Complementing these three strategies were a number of school structures and systems which the heads had put in place and which I have outlined above. These structures were both support mechanisms and different media for conveying the educational messages the heads wanted to see adopted in the schools.

Together, the leadership strategies, organisational and curricular structures and systems were the processes by which shared educational values and goals were created, the ways in which consistency in teaching and high expectations were put in place and the means by which improvements in pupils' learning outcomes and progress were achieved.

Leadership

Without doubt these heads were leading their schools: no one dissented from this view. The previous sections have provided evidence to support these claims and illustrations of how they actually went about leading their schools. This study has thus begun to describe the anatomy of successful leadership in small primary schools. Everything these heads did was concentrated on enhancing pupils' learning provision, progress and outcomes and was performed in an educative way. In developing the quality of learning the heads frequently enabled staff to learn from them as teachers and also from one another. Thus the process of improvement was most often a learning process for the staff.

The heads focused strongly and directly on improving the quality of teaching. They looked hard at how children were being taught and considered how such practice might be improved and shared so that every teacher could teach to the same standard as the best. Much of this development in pedagogy occurred through modelling, monitoring and discussion, with all three strategies being predicated on teachers being able to learn with and from one another. Thus improving teaching was based on professional learning. What all this adds up to is the fact that these heads were both educational and educative leaders.

Yet these heads were not 'hero leaders' single-handedly transforming their schools. Some had worked like that for a period of time, but all now worked with their colleagues. Moreover, 'best practice' in management outside education is presently pointing towards 'liberating leadership' with a focus on trust, integrity, fairness and belief in self and others (Turner 1998). As Glatter (1999) has suggested, effective human resource management practices contribute far more, in statistical terms, to company performance than do strategy, quality, technology and research and development combined:

> The increasing emphasis on people management is reflected in the growing literature on the significance in modern conditions of the 'intellectual capital' of organisations (e.g. Allday 1998, Stewart 1998), with its implications for valuing, motivating and developing staff.
>
> (Glatter 1999)

The ten heads in this study provided educational leadership in ways that enabled staff to feel involved and respected their participation. They were effective managers and leaders of people because they motivated their staff and valued their professional craft knowledge about teaching, learning and children by treating them as colleagues and partners.

Professional development

How these heads came to terms with the role and the particular challenges they faced was by learning on the job. Thus it may be important for anyone appointed to a headship to be able to be a continuing professional learner: that is, someone who is able to solve the myriad 'problems' they encounter, is sufficiently flexible to think their way round obstacles and difficulties, is positive and proactive and capable of working things out for themselves and by themselves as well as with others. Heads need to be active, reflective learners who able to work out independently how to deal with all the problems, issues and challenges they encounter in the course of their work. In this way their work is a course of study and they need to be students of that work.

Conclusions

This research throws into relief a number of issues. It demonstrates that headship is concerned with several major skills and knowledge areas: interpersonal leadership, self-management, learning, teaching and the professional development of both one's staff and oneself. Though these findings are not new, the research shows how such skills are understood by heads, teachers and governors. Moreover, the study suggests that when used effectively they exert a positive influence on teachers and other stakeholders. Thus the portrait offered here is not simply a description of headship by heads of small schools; it is also an analytical account of what the leaders and followers find influential. In other words, this is an outline of 'what works' in terms of heads exercising social influence upon colleagues and others.

These concluding points will be returned to later. In the meantime it is important to consider headship in medium- and large-sized primary schools, which will be discussed in the following two chapters.

3 Leadership in medium-sized primary schools

This chapter concentrates on leadership in medium sized primary school. The project which provides the data for the findings and interpretation offered here was the 'Heads in Essex Leadership Programme' (HELP), which I co-directed with Paul Lincoln, then Director of Learning Services, Essex County Council. We had worked together on the Essex Primary School Improvement programme in the mid-1990s (see Southworth and Lincoln 1999) and wished to follow that up with a specific examination of leadership in improving primary schools. When the Esmée Fairbairn Foundation advertised for project proposals for their 'Heads You Win' programme we developed a submission and were delighted when it was accepted and funded.

The chapter is divided into five sections. Details of the project are set out in the next section. The second, third and fourth sections look at the project findings under the headings of: leadership; structures and systems; and impacting on children's achievements. These three sections cover the main insights that emerge from the project, while the fifth draws together the main themes and conclusions.

Aims and methods

HELP was designed to look at leadership in primary schools facing challenging circumstances and where there was evidence of sustained improvement in pupils' achievements. The project was funded by the Esmée Fairbairn Foundation and one of twelve projects the Foundation supported as part of its 'Heads You Win' programme. This programme sought to encourage a spirit of self-development and improvement for head teachers in the primary sector. The focus on primary heads came about because the Foundation believed these heads had fewer opportunities for reflection and development than their colleagues in secondary schools and wanted to address this imbalance (see Esmée Fairbairn Foundation 2001).

Recognising that both leadership in schools and pupil achievement and progress matter, HELP aimed to explore the links between the two. We set out to organise a collaborative enquiry in which all the project participants worked together to develop a body of detailed, practical knowledge about leading improving primary schools. The project aims were to:

- Identify head teachers whose schools had made the greatest improvement in pupil outcomes in challenging circumstances;
- Enable these head teachers to analyse the ways in which they led and managed their schools' improvements;
- Encourage the head teachers to apply their collective knowledge of leading improving schools to enhance pupil outcomes further, support their deputies' development and share their ideas with other schools;
- Value the work of head teachers and schools who are having an impact on pupil achievement which is not currently recognised by league tables.

We took an open-ended approach to the research in that while we were clear about what we wanted to look at we were aware that the focus would shift over time and in the light of emerging issues and insights. We also wanted to make the enquiry as flexible and responsive to the heads' ideas as we could. Nevertheless, we did have a structure and timetable for the project since we wanted the heads to know when we would all be working together so that they could manage their time and commitments and thus be available to participate.

Once all the schools – nineteen in all – had been identified and the invited heads had agreed to participate, we held an initial briefing to launch the project. Then each term, for three terms, we hosted a twenty-four-hour residential workshop where we concentrated on particular issues. In the first one we looked at how the heads led their schools, and from this emerged the focus of the second: the use of structures and systems in their schools. The third and final workshop reviewed the ideas we had developed, refined them and identified further questions. In between these residential workshops the heads met with us for single-day seminars where we followed up the residential workshops by reflecting on the outcomes. The heads also undertook some tasks framed by the group. These were individual, short, written tasks which were used to inform discussion and group work and which Paul and I also read and analysed. The heads wrote about the following topics:

- How they led their schools;
- What structures, systems and processes they had put in place to bring about school improvement;
- What their action plans were for the project year and for the following year;
- How they shared their leadership with others in the school;
- What they believed had made the most difference to enhancing pupil outcomes;
- What they had learned from working together.

In between the scheduled meetings of participants the two programme leaders met regularly to plan the activities in detail, summarise and analyse the reports the heads had written and write up our ideas and interpretations of these data sets. These summaries and analyses were always shared with the group, to whose critical appraisal everything produced was subjected.

The project produced a wealth of material. Nineteen heads writing and talking about how they led, orchestrated and organised their schools' improvement efforts generated a host of ideas, all of them grounded in the heads' day-to-day practice and the fruit of their deep professional knowledge and understanding.

However, it was not always easy or straightforward to produce this material. For one thing, the heads were accustomed to 'doing school improvement' rather than talking and writing about it. Thus initially they found talking about their work rather awkward. Over time and through small-group work and paired activities their inhibitions decreased and their articulateness increased.

The schools which the LEA identified and which agreed to participate covered a range of school sizes: the smallest had ninety-eight pupils on roll and the largest 502. As the table below shows, apart from these two and one other with 121 pupils on roll, the rest fell into the 150–330 range, thus straddling the national average size of primary schools in England which is, according to DFES provisional data 242.6 (DFES 2002). The average size of these nineteen schools is 194.

Table 3.1 Size of schools in HELP project

School	Number of pupils	Number of staff
1	98	6
2	126	7
3	151	8
4	163	8
5	164	7
6	179	9
7	184	9
8	185	11
9	196	9
10	233	10
11	234	9
12	258	12
13	263	11
14	266	10
15	285	13
16	317	16
17	323	16
18	331	15
19	502	19

Note: The variations in ratio of staff to pupils are accounted for by the number of part-time staff counted in as opposed to full-time teachers. Thus while School 8 apparently has more staff but fewer pupils than School 9, the former has more part-time teachers than the latter.

Source: Project data.

Findings

The heads shared numerous stories about their schools' development, the changes they had seen take place and the issues they were still facing. Although it is not possible to present here all that we found out, I can reveal much of the material, and in the following sections I shall concentrate on three areas:

- Leadership;
- Structures and systems;
- Impact on children's achievements.

Leadership in medium-sized, improving schools: categories and characteristics

Following group discussions and individual writing tasks we were able to develop a category analysis of the heads' leadership. The categories we initially developed from the heads' testimonies were:

- Personal qualities
- Professional focus
- Structures and systems
- Using initiatives and projects
- External links
- Awareness of challenge and change
- Contexts and situations
- Leadership
- Tackling underperformance.

I shall now expand on each of these categories in turn.

Much was made in many of the heads' reports of *personal qualities* such as treating people fairly and with respect and being honest and open (although some also admitted to not always being open and to keeping things to themselves). Listening to and sensitivity to others were qualities also noted in many of the reports. Such emphases suggest that these heads regarded school leadership as strongly person-centred. They were all aware that leadership involved an interpersonal dimension. At the same time, their remarks implied that it was a moral and ethical activity. Treating people fairly and equitably were points made repeatedly throughout the project, and the ideal of living out these values was one they all aspired to. Moreover, when individual heads felt they had acted in a way that breached their personal ethical code, this troubled them considerably and – to judge by what they said – left them feeling either disappointed with themselves or guilty.

At one point a group of heads produced a paper which addressed the question: What sort of people are we? In it they set down the common characteristics they saw for all or nearly all those participating in the project. The points they listed are set out in Table 3.2:

Table 3.2 Personal characteristics of heads in HELP project

'People' people, not 'paper' people	Ability to multitask	Value structures and systems
Passionate about our jobs	Show empathy	Seek perfection
Ability to switch leadership styles	Use statistics [data on pupils' attainment],	'We are learners and accept change'
Value training	especially benchmarking Not satisfied with being average	Ordinary, down-to-earth people
Bored very easily	Risk-takers	Accurate self-image

Source: Project data.

These points reinforce several of the interpretations already raised or preface issues discussed later in this section. For example, the idea that the heads were 'people' people, not 'paper' people' is another way of saying they were person-centred.

The individually written reports showed that each head was *professionally focused*. Most telling was the emphasis on pupils' learning as well as on the quality of teaching, on curricular provision for pupils and on the wish to know what was happening inside classrooms. Although several heads were concerned about the narrowness of pupil learning-outcome measures, many of them had nevertheless been 'stimulated' by SATs results, school inspection findings and other data which showed how well (or otherwise) the school was performing. The heads used outcome and process 'data' to identify and formulate plans for future action. Indeed, information from a variety of sources was used by them to establish school improvement priorities. Thus an important area of professional focus was the intention to improve the school's levels of performance and to sustain these improvements over time.

Many references were made to organisational, curricular and staff support *systems and structures*. As noted in the table above, the heads valued structures and systems. These included monitoring, meetings, roles, senior management teams (SMTs), delegation, special educational needs (SEN), special needs coordinators' (SENCOs) roles, policies, planning (teachers and head teacher), school review, evaluation, appraisal, target setting, feedback, staff selection, staff handbooks, teacher release time, teamwork, staff development, the deployment of learning support staff (LSAs) and the use of evidence to inform decision-making. So strong was the emphasis the heads placed on these structures and systems that we agreed it should be explored in some depth and hence this category is examined further in the next sub-section.

A number of heads stated (and others implied) that they had taken advantage of a range of external initiatives to support their schools' improvement efforts. Others had developed their own internal projects to support their schools' development. In other words, certain change-related projects were being used as vehicles for improving the school. Examples included: the implementation of the national literacy and numeracy strategies; the introduction of computer suites into schools to develop ICT across the curriculum; the building of links with local nursery schools; classroom observation and monitoring activities performed by the head, senior staff or peers; the introduction of whole-school approaches to self-evaluation; the Early Reading Research Project, which the LEA was sponsoring; the developing of positive pupil-behaviour programmes; the use of subject specialist teaching in Years 5 and 6; the provision of 'key experiences' for children; involvement in the Essex Primary School Improvement Programme (EPSI); becoming part of a local Education Action Zone.

Running across a good proportion of the reports was a sense of the value of *external relations* and the need to keep aware of what was happening in the environment. The involvement of parents and governors was often mentioned. In many cases, developments had either taken or were taking place. Several heads mentioned that they had links with the community; while other schools had partnership arrangements with institutions of higher education.

Following on from the previous set of points, many heads demonstrated their *awareness of external change* mandates and the need to keep abreast of what was happening elsewhere in education, with the DfES cited on a number of occasions. Keeping up with successive change was a challenge. It was apparent from a number of the reports that change and the need for it arose from different sources. Heads who were relatively new to their schools may have wanted to alter and develop things because they felt the school needed improving in some respect or other. Some longer-serving heads, however, also realised that existing arrangements and school practices needed to be altered. OFSTED was mentioned with reference to the latter, but so too were SATs results and other indicators and self-evaluation data.

This attention to the external environment reveals these heads' awareness of the contexts in which they were working. They knew that the policy environment was something they needed to heed. However, much the stronger sense of context came from their awareness of the school as an organisation as well as its levels of performance, the staff's strengths, skills and development needs, the school's history, the needs of individuals and teams and the teacher/staff cultures. These things showed that all were acutely aware of *the school as a context* for their leadership. The sense that the school was the head's 'theatre of operation' was very strong. It was their major preoccupation and interest, and all were able to talk at length and in great depth about 'their' schools. It filled their minds and absorbed them fully.

The heads were also very self-aware. Personal comments about their professional and personal values and beliefs were made, as were statements about the length of time in post and the possible effects of longevity. These suggest awareness of role maturity, professional development and the need to remain motivated. They showed that they knew their individual situations were another factor in the dynamics of the school and its development.

Many statements emerged around the theme of 'How I lead'. The following points drawn from the heads' accounts convey how they saw themselves as leaders and what *leadership* meant for them:

- Creating the conditions for success and improvement;
- Providing opportunities for staff to perform and lead and for pupils to learn;
- Influencing colleagues – *not* telling them;
- Mediating – working with and through others;
- Hands-on; in touch; MBWA (managing and monitoring by wandering about); being visible;
- Modelling;
- Pace-setting;
- Being organised;
- Positive reinforcement;
- Being optimistic.

In a number of cases pupil, school and/or teacher underperformance were mentioned. There were also references to low teacher expectations being raised and the need for more explicit emphases being placed on standards, progress and success. What these comments suggested was the heads' willingness to confront poor or unsatisfactory levels of performance and do something about it. They all knew they had to hold colleagues to account and that, as heads, they had to *tackle underperformance*. It was plain from working with them that many had already confronted underperformance – be it institutional or individual – and that in the process of confronting these deficiencies they had shown their colleagues and others that there were thresholds below which they were not prepared to tolerate poor or unsatisfactory practice.

When this category analysis of their leadership had been delineated, the heads were invited to contrast them with another which the Hay Group had developed for the DfES on performance management. The Hay Group identified eighteen categories in an attempt to outline effective school leadership characteristics, and these eighteen are listed in Appendix 1. One important aspect of this analysis was the stress Hay placed on the categories being interrelated and working in combinations. The Hay Group granted us permission to share these in order that the heads could comment on their appropriateness. Over the course of three months the heads used the Hay Group categories and later commented on their general applicability. They found them useful as an analytical tool and generally agreed that they had validity.

Such lists are, of course, of limited use. They are at best outlines of what heads say they do. Also, as we were all aware, they tend to emphasise the similarities and ignore the differences between individuals. One of the striking features of the accounts the heads produced and of their discussions was the fact that they were very different, as well as having certain professional characteristics in common. Members of the group frequently stressed that there was considerable variation in their approaches to leadership. Thus one of the main characteristics of school leadership is variety. There is no single best way to lead; there are many pathways to success.

MacBeath and Myers (1999) express much the same point when they say:

> With the arrival of the new headteacher, schools can 'turn around' and move from disaster to triumph. Losses are turned into gains. Low achievement becomes high achievement. The new head knows what to do to put things right because there is an unwritten rulebook of good, even 'best' practice.
>
> Viewed from a distance, this seems to describe what actually happens, and both the gloss in the literature and the rhetoric of the politician endorse that neat and tidy state of the art. Yet head teachers who have had an impact on schools tell a different story. The Effective Leadership Study (MacBeath 1998) which included forty heads from four countries, explored the anxiety, the stress, the difficult choices – the human side of leadership. It failed to find a golden rulebook or recipe for effective leadership, but did identify ways of increasing our understanding of – and response to – dilemmas.
>
> (MacBeath and Myers 1999, p. 67).

Indeed, the search for a single, winning leadership formula, or a 'genetic blueprint' may be a blind alley, because there are no traits which apply to all leaders. Moreover, all the evidence from a hundred years of research into leadership suggests that there is no single set of skills. Leadership is dependent upon context, as noted in Chapter 1, but worth repeating here in greater detail:

> ... productive leadership depends heavily on its fit with the social and organisational context in which it is exercised. So, as times change, what works for leaders changes also.
>
> This is not to deny that there are relatively enduring leadership qualities – qualities that travel well through time and across organisational contexts ... [but] there is no final word on what is good leadership. We are simply trying to hit a moving target; maybe even get a little ahead of it. Granted, the qualities that are relatively enduring may become clearer in the process, but these qualities will never be more than the 'basic skills' of leadership. They will never tell us anything important about how to exercise outstanding leadership, because outstanding leadership is exquisitely sensitive to the context in which it is exercised.
>
> (Leithwood, Jantzi and Steinbach 1999: 3–4)

The common characteristics identified in this chapter, then, are but a sketch of leadership; colour, texture and pattern still need to be applied to the sketch, and this is where individual differences come into play. We might be able to trace the outlines, but it is individuals who provide the tone, shade and highlights.

Further reflections on the characteristics, to which we returned from time to time, helped us to refine the lists further. In the light of our early efforts and the

Hay Group's work, we settled on a concise set of common characteristics relating to effective school leadership:

- *Drive*: determined; clear-sighted, sense of direction; high expectations; will to succeed; purposeful; principled; conviction; single-minded (at times); competitive; hard-working; achievement-oriented; dislike of failure or lack of success/progress; wants to make a difference; positive; relentless; tenacious; focused; anticipates change.
- *Improvement-focused*: wants to improve; make things better; believes things can be better; pushing for improvements; wants best for children/staff/parents/ school; intolerant of poor performance; belief in success for all; positive behaviour; sees opportunities; monitors; analyses; uses data; self-evaluation; target-setting and targeted actions; outcome-oriented; needs-based; context-specific; restless; uses external change for internal improvement.
- *Highly organised*: designs and develops structures, systems and processes; action planning; little left to chance; uses time carefully; multi-task.
- *Hands-on leadership*: action-oriented; involved; gets things done; task-completer; uses what works; flexible; interventionist; works around barriers/obstacles; knows what is going on; monitors/management by wandering about (MBWA); perceives parts and the whole.
- *Works with others*: shared leadership (though not always); team-oriented; aware of others; empathetic; inclusive; quality relationships; morale-raising; supportive; developmental; recognises ideas and initiatives; positive reinforcement; 'no blame' cultures; aware of group dynamics; micro-political; tough, pragmatic; educative/learner; adaptive – uses variety of styles; talk is the work; medium is the message; direct and indirect in dealing with staff; energy-creators.

Although there is much to discuss and expand on here, this set of categories and characteristics comes closest to recording what the heads themselves said. The categories may constitute what Leithwood and his associates (1999) call the 'basic skills' of leadership.

The classification suggests that the heads concentrated on school improvement by using a range of strategies and tactics. First, they were intrinsically motivated by their professional beliefs. They believed children and teachers could succeed and wanted the very best for the schools they led. Success meant getting better – making progress – that is, moving the school, including all who work there, forward. To achieve this the heads were highly organised. Indeed, in some there seemed to be an addiction to organisation! They employed a combination of processes, hands-on leadership, support, pressure and challenge. They worked hard at building teams, motivating colleagues and developing staff morale. They also remained classroom- and pupil-focused, were visible in the school and monitored pupil outcomes, achievements and progress. Many, though not all, taught on a regular basis (e.g. literacy groups each day, cover teaching to release staff, planned teaching sessions each week). Although the heads mostly emphasised how they supported staff, many also noted that on occasion they could also be tough if necessary. They did not tolerate poor performance from colleagues.

One other set of characteristics also needs to be added: as a group these heads were very modest. They avoided extravagant claims about their success as leaders, preferring instead to cite the efforts of others. Indeed, they presented themselves as ordinary heads and did not see their actions as particularly remarkable.

The categories also helped us to identify certain areas of leadership on which we needed greater information. One of these was shared leadership, and consequently the heads were asked to write about this. The following subsection reports on what emerged from their accounts.

Shared leadership

All the heads either believed or hoped that they shared leadership with school colleagues. Two sets of colleagues were commonly noted as people with whom leadership was shared: the deputy head and the senior management team (SMT). The latter were often mentioned, sometimes more than the deputy alone, although the deputy was always a member of the SMT. The frequency with which the SMT was mentioned is itself significant. Ten years ago it is unlikely that such a group of heads would have made reference to a senior management team, today, they are much more common in primary schools.

In terms of the deputy heads, the following comments traced their involvement in leadership:

- *The deputy leads on a number of identified priorities including curriculum development issues arising from the post-OFSTED action plan, monitoring progress across Key Stage 1 and parent partnerships.*
- *The deputy leads in aspects of the curriculum, planning and assessment where credibility is important and where an exemplar of good practice is essential.*
- *The deputy has responsibility for ensuring the effectiveness of curriculum coordinators.*
- *The deputy has a specific role in school development – to develop and monitor assessment and record-keeping.*

Asked about how the heads followed when other colleagues led, the heads commented that:

- *[I follow] by being the same as everyone else when someone leads – having respect for others' views and knowing I cannot and do not know it all.*
- *When colleagues lead INSET I take the same role as other members of staff as far as possible. I am in a learning role just as much as everyone else.*
- *If someone else is leading an INSET session or staff meeting, for example, I am a 'learner' – taking notes, asking questions, receiving handouts. I take part in all practical activities.*

Some, however, acknowledged the challenge of being a head and a follower, saying, for example:

- *This is the most difficult question! I like to think I follow and demonstrate followership. I think I do it by listening, being open-minded, not conveying the impression that only my opinion is to be valued.*

These comments suggest that the heads were involving their deputies and members of the SMT in monitoring, data analysis and school self-evaluation activities.

When the heads were asked about how much release time deputies and other school leaders received, it was found that they all ensured that these colleagues had some non-contact time. This varied from school to school and was often dependent upon the roles and responsibilities of individuals within each school's organisational structures. Some of the heads expressed concern about not having enough money to fund adequate levels of release time. Deputies received between a half and one day a week non-contact time in many of the schools. SENCOs were also cited in some as receiving non-contact time, as were coordinators responsible for core subjects (literacy, maths, science).

Release time was most commonly used for monitoring work. For example:

- *The deputy has one day per week to monitor, support, observe, work on agreed target and work with me.*

Overall, the information provided about shared leadership suggests that the project heads were involving other colleagues. Deputies were most frequently cited, but so too were SMT members.

A few of the heads expressed concerns about 'letting go'. One or two found it hard to devolve leadership, either because it caused them some discomfort or because of a lack of confidence in those to whom they were delegating. Nevertheless, the overwhelming impression from the heads' replies is that they were delegating to others, that leadership and management were shared and, in particular, that deputies played a role in improving their schools. The single most important role for other leaders appeared to be monitoring. Deputies, senior teachers and coordinators were examining samples of pupils' books, observing lessons and classrooms and looking at pupil learning data.

Structures and systems in the schools

The information the heads supplied about the organisational, curricular and staff development structures and systems they used in their schools was particularly detailed and valuable. The heads were asked to report on the structures and systems they used under the following headings:

1   Use of staff;
2   Planning;
3   Monitoring;
4   Use of evidence/data;
5   Use of meetings;
6   Training.

These headings were adopted with the agreement of the group after early work in the project suggested there was more to explore here. However, many of the heads refined these headings and developed others when reporting on the systems in use in their schools.

Examples of four heads' descriptions of their respective schools' structures and systems are presented in Appendix 2. These were chosen because together they cover the great majority of items which all the heads listed and because they offer details of the particular structures and systems in these schools. Not only do they make for interesting reading but also they are a resource for heads and deputies in similar schools to look at and contrast with their own schools' systems, as well as being an indication for prospective leaders in medium-sized schools of the kinds of things they might need to put in place.

Within the headings the group agreed to use as a format for their reports, a number of other common elements emerged. For example, under the 'use of staff' heading much was said about deputies, curriculum coordinators/subject leaders and SENCOs. A majority of the heads also stressed the value and importance of support staff. Midday assistants and classroom support staff were identified as having particular needs, and many of the heads had ensured there were clear job descriptions and lines of communication as well as development opportunities for them.

Similarly, there were many common approaches to planning in these schools. Teachers were encouraged to plan in pairs or teams while school development plans were more akin to 'corporate plans' than 'singular plans' (MacGilchrist *et al.* 1995: 134–5). Singular plans are those owned by head teachers alone; whereas corporate plans are characterised by 'a united effort to improve' (p. 195). They reflect a strong sense of shared ownership and involvement on the part of the teaching staff, and attempts are made to include others in the process too. There is also a focus on teaching and learning, especially on improvements in the quality of pupils' learning, while links can be seen between school and teacher development and pupils' development. For example, one of the heads wrote, under the heading 'Planning mechanisms':

> School development plan (SDP) is discussed with all staff and governors. All staff make a contribution.
> SDP is informed by teaching and non-teaching staff training and development audit.
> All coordinators complete action plans for their subject areas.
> All year-group heads complete action plans for their year groups.
> Staff development plan informs SDP.

The heads' reports also validated a number of the points made earlier in this chapter. First, they showed how organised the heads were. In addition they demonstrated how strongly focused the heads were on school improvement, pupils' learning and progress and the growth of the school as an organisation. The structures and systems were underscored by an intention to create and sustain the school as a developing organisation. Some of the structures and systems did serve bureaucratic purposes, but most were intended to enable staff to work together, share their ideas, priorities and concerns and to grow both as individuals and members of the group. There was an educative intent at work, namely to make as many of the systems as possible opportunities for individuals to learn with and from others. Thus, signals emerged about staff working along-side others, finding out what each individual was doing, drawing on expertise wherever it resided and sharing professional knowledge and experience.

This developmental intention also relates to the kinds of staff cultures that existed in these schools. From what we heard and knew about these schools, the heads appeared to favour collaborative staff cultures. It also seems that they used the organisational, curricular and staff development structures to build and sustain such cultures. They understood – either explicitly or implicitly – that each and every one of the systems they developed played a part in culture development in the school. We know from research into organisational cultures that structures and systems do play a part in creating, sustaining or destroying staff cultures (Schein 1985, Deal and Kennedy 1988, Rosenholtz 1989, Fullan and Hargreaves 1992, Deal and Peterson 1999). These heads knew this too, thus each particular structure or system was not seen as a separate piece of the school; rather it was understood to fit into a larger pattern and purpose.

This idea, in turn, tells us something about the heads' leadership abilities. It shows that the heads had an eye for detail and were also able to see the bigger picture. Moreover, they could see the relationship between individual parts and the whole. Being able to perceive and think about how elements interrelate and integrate is essential to having a sense of 'whole school', since this notion rests on leaders being able to have a perceptual and intellectual sense of holism. Thus what is suggested here is that these heads used the organisational, curricular and staff development structures and systems in an integrative way. The particular aspects of the schools' operations combined to make each school a cohesive organisation in which development and collaboration were logical outcomes of all the systems.

While leaders and head teachers in all schools need to be able to have a sense of the school being a united, integrated entity – a 'whole' school – the larger the school, the more this becomes an imperative and key skill. In smaller schools the task is important, but it is not as complex. In medium-sized and larger schools it grows in both complexity and significance. That is probably why it has emerged more strongly in this chapter than in the previous one. There is a real need for heads and other leaders to transcend their classroom perspectives, to see beyond the detail and develop the ability to understand how various pieces relate to one another and go to make up a unified whole.

Use of the head's time

We also asked the heads to look at how they used time. Their accounts showed that time management represented a challenge, not least because their days were characterised by brevity, variety and fragmentation. There were many unexpected demands on their time. To counteract this daily pattern they tried to plan ahead, set priorities for themselves and aimed to protect themselves from too many interruptions or distractions.

However, many of the reports showed that despite all the care, foresight and planning these heads applied to their work and their schools, the role is, on a day-to-day basis, typified by flexibility, responsiveness and multiple demands. There is a great deal to attend to and so much to remain forever aware of. Sometimes just keeping the school running was a big enough task; trying to move the school forward and ensuring that the movement was an improvement was even harder, particularly in the contexts in which these schools were operating. In other words – and in harmony with the previous chapter – headship in medium-sized schools involved tireless commitment, the capacity to multi-task and the mental ability and agility to retain many things in one's mind at once. Headship in these schools was plainly hard work, and while these heads had an appetite for such effort, even they confessed to becoming tired towards the end of each term.

Changes which had the most impact on children's achievements

We all agreed during the project that it would be revealing to know what each head thought about the changes they had made and how they had impacted on the classrooms and the school's improvement. Eventually we settled on this question as the stimulus for the group's reflections: '*What are the changes you have made that you think have had the most impact on children's achievements?*'

The heads' responses to this question ranged from the more intangible cultural changes, such as building self-esteem and introducing a 'can do' culture, to the very specific introduction of a new approach such as the Early Reading Research Project.

The heads' responses were grouped into categories which are listed below with a descriptor of what the category covered and the number of participants who judged it to have had an impact on pupil achievement.

- Constantly developing the *quality of the teaching staff* which included recruitment, deployment, building teams, training, and the use of staff time.   11
- *Monitoring systems* which clarified, reinforced and gave feedback on standards and expectations, including classroom observation.   10
- *Curriculum planning* and assessment which included medium and short-term plans, whole school systems and the use of time. The emphasis was on 'improving', 'tightening up', 'focus', 'more rigorous'.   9
- *Use of data* and *target-setting* for a purpose: to monitor progress, to prove children could achieve more.   9
- *Positive behaviour management.*   9

- *Special Educational Needs developments* including appointment of SENCO with release time, SENCO development, staff training, early identification and provision, better use of assessment and individual programmes.   5
- *Essex Early Reading Research*. This was the only change mentioned where participants described a direct correlation with increased pupil achievement.   5
- Celebrating achievement, developing a *'can-do' culture* including the impact on raising self-esteem amongst staff and children alike.   5
- *Teaching and learning* which included how children learn, developing independent learning, pupil grouping and classroom organisation.   5
- *Parental involvement*, which included better communications.   4
- *School development planning* with a focus on forward thinking, staff involvement, and monitoring progress.   4
- *Literacy and numeracy strategies*.   4
- *Early years and nursery provision*.   2
- *Resources and the environment* including their use and improvement.   2
- *Learning assistants*, their deployment and development.   2

That the quality of teaching staff is paramount here came as no surprise. It echoes what the heads of the small schools said and is a theme taken up in Chapters 5 and 7 as well. This high rating also reinforces the importance of finding, recruiting and retaining high-quality teachers. Much the same issue has been noted in the business and management sector. Research into businesses which had moved from being 'good' to 'great' companies in performance terms found that they had all devoted time, effort and energy to finding the best people they could. In part this was because these successful companies understood that people are the most important part of the organisation. Yet the author of this study, refines this idea by stating: 'In a good-to-great transformation, people are not your most important asset. The *right* people are.' (Collins 2001: 51).

A number of the heads who participated in the HELP project were developing more sophisticated selection strategies than just an interview. They were also devoting great care to team-building, training and the use of release time. In a sense, having got the right people on the team they then made as much use of them as they could across the school as well as in the classroom. Selection is obviously important, but once staff have been recruited, they need to be retained. Staff retention involves identifying their development needs and meeting them, providing them with new opportunities and challenges and deploying their expertise and skills to maximum effect so that they feel their skills are recognised, valued and utilised. Many of the heads in this project knew this and did so.

Curriculum planning and assessment, monitoring systems including classroom observation and the use of data for target-setting all scored highly. This reinforces the findings which emerged from the Essex Primary School Improvement (EPSI) programme (Southworth and Lincoln 1999), namely that the formal model of school improvement, involving careful planning, implementation, monitoring and school review, has a positive impact on raising the level of pupil achievement.

In the EPSI project we concluded that an emphasis on the informal cultural aspects of improvement, in conjunction with the formal model, had even greater impact and was more likely to ensure sustainability. This was echoed by the head teachers in this study, who placed importance on celebrating achievement, raising staff and pupils, self-esteem and developing a 'can do' culture. In other words, the structures and systems they applied provided a formal framework in which staff worked, but this was accompanied by informal ways of working which were in harmony with the formal tactics and which supplemented and enriched those structures and systems.

Schools participating in the HELP research project were chosen specifically because of their success in raising achievement in challenging circumstances. Therefore it should not be surprising that these head teachers placed a strong emphasis on establishing both positive behaviour-management systems and effective procedures for the identification of and provision for children with special educational needs. These developments were motivated by two principles: the first, that it is essential to have an ordered environment with good behaviour if children are to learn; and the second, that if teachers are effective in differentiating the curriculum for those with the greatest learning difficulties, then they can similarly do it for all children, thereby ensuring good progress for all pupils.

The 'formal' model of school improvement as argued above undoubtedly raises pupil achievement. Schools, like those in this programme, who have adopted these strategies and brought about significant improvement will, however, eventually plateau. It is at this point that renewed attention needs to be paid to what is happening in the classroom and, in particular, to teaching which reflects how children learn. This was implied by the head teachers who cited the Early Reading Research, the national literacy and numeracy strategies and a focus on teaching and learning including the developing of independent learning and pupil grouping. What was going on in these schools was a deeper and more sustained attention to improvement. Having begun to raise standards of achievement, the heads knew that it was important to build on this by strengthening and developing the quality of teaching to further enhance levels of achievement. Thus they used initiatives in literacy and numeracy to simultaneously develop the quality of teaching, putting into practice what others have argued for some time: that schools will not improve unless the quality of teaching changes for the better (Galton 1995, Southworth 1996).

It was interesting that four participants rated improved parental involvement highly in its impact on pupil achievement. Involving parents in their children's learning – particularly those living in more disadvantaged areas – can obviously be significant, but it is also challenging. We were not able to explore exactly what had happened in these schools. Therefore more attention needs to be focused on identifying, investigating and spreading those strategies that have proved successful.

Lastly, the point needs to be made that perhaps the most important element of this part of the project was the question rather than the answers. Important, interesting and intriguing as these heads' responses are, it may be equally important for all leaders in each and every school to ask the question of themselves and then share their answers to it. The question may well be an important resource to school leaders wishing to examine how their schools are improving and why.

Conclusions

In concluding this chapter, four major themes stand out, and it is on these that I will now focus.

Effective headship in medium-sized schools demands individuals who have drive and determination

Headship is hard work, for all the reasons identified in this and the previous chapter, but also because this sample of heads worked in schools that faced challenging circumstances. A comparable study was conducted into headship in similar schools in the mid-1990s. That study, 'Success Against the Odds' (NCE 1996), looked at effective schools in disadvantaged areas and concluded that leadership and management in the studied schools required leaders with an 'abundance of energy and commitment' and that there was 'an unusually high level of human effort being spent in a very focused way' (p. 335). The NCE study also highlighted the fact that the heads exercised their leadership by 'being about the school' and kept a high profile, getting to know the pupils, following their progress and spending time observing teaching and learning (p. 337). These observations are echoed in this chapter. The heads plainly worked hard, had lots of energy, were focused on learning and teaching and knew their schools inside out.

The NCE study also analysed the personal styles of the heads they encountered, and the study summarised them thus:

> In each case the vision of the headteacher is a pervasive and influential force, but the individual is not necessarily a dominating character. Their drive is essentially positive, confident and pro-active, supported by clear objectives, but not imposed on staff against their will . . . 'The overriding impression of the headteacher is one of irresistible cheerfulness in a low key and unobtrusive way.'
>
> The word 'understated' is used in the accounts much more frequently than 'charismatic'.
>
> (NCE 1996: 339)

This statement has much in common with the picture painted in this chapter. The heads were approachable, 'quiet' rather than 'noisy' leaders, keen to involve others, led by example and were powerful role models. They put a great deal of time, effort and energy into their work and were fascinated by it. Their determination to succeed was driven by a fear of failure: none of them liked to be defeated and many told me they wanted to show that children who came from disadvantaged backgrounds could succeed every bit as much as those who enjoyed more advantaged material and social settings. These heads worked as they did because they wanted to do the very best they could for the children.

The heads were person-centred leaders

Like their counterparts in the small schools, these heads knew that they worked with and through colleagues. Hence much was made of collaboration, the staff being a team and the need to build and develop this team. When they were able to appoint staff, time and care were taken to find the right people, but this was followed up with equal attention to induction and to developing the newly appointed individuals, and also making use of the skills and talents that had won them the job.

While valuing and recognising individuals, the heads also knew they had to create consistency across the school. Therefore they had designed and implemented a range of organisational, curricular and staff-development structures and systems that provided a common framework for all staff members to work within. They aimed to establish and sustain a unity of purpose for the staff through agreed ground rules and procedures. In this way they sought to secure the best from individuals and from the team of which they were members.

Shared leadership

Here the role of the deputy is prominent in ways which were not as noticeable in the previous chapter. There are several reasons why shared leadership emerges here to the degree it does. For one thing, many small schools do not have a deputy. For another, as the size of the school increases, heads need to share out the management and leadership load. Hence these heads of medium-sized schools wanted to work in partnership with their deputy-head colleagues. Some also included other senior staff in a senior management team. Thus shared leadership extended in some cases to more than one other individual working alongside the head.

Teacher and staff cultures

These heads were implicitly aware of the need to develop and sustain a staff culture that supported their ambitions for the schools. They recognised that they and other key staff needed to create and sustain a set of ways of working which enabled staff to operate productively together for the good of the children, themselves and the school as a whole including all its stakeholders.

Collaboration was an important element of this culture, as I argued above, but on further reflection, and when many of the ideas in this chapter are pieced together, it seems there was evidence that these heads had transcended earlier notions of teacher cultures of collaboration (Nias *et al.* 1989) and developed cultures of improvement.

Collaboration was valued because it helped staff to work together in ways that allowed them to develop. Also, it fostered a sense of 'whole school' and a unity of purpose. However, working together was not an end in itself; it was a means to another end, namely the growth and improvement of the school. This 'culture of improvement' appeared, on the evidence of these heads' testimonies, to be one which is:

- Outcome-focused
- Process-oriented
- Emphasises improvement is the responsibility of all
- Promotes high expectations of pupils, colleagues and self
- Collaborative
- Inclusive – teachers, LSAs, pupils, governors, parents
- Supports teacher learning and development
- Formally organised with clear structures and systems
- Self-evaluatory
- Connected to classrooms
- Concerned to support pupil learning and the quality of teaching.

Moreover, the heads worked to create such a culture through formal and informal means. The structures and systems which have figured prominently in this chapter were designed to promote ways of working and values and beliefs concerning the nature of professional work in primary schools today. The structures and systems embody and project a sense that the school needs to keep on improving, growing and developing. This is achieved by looking carefully at what is happening, by analysing pupil progress and achievement data, and by leaders reflecting the message that everyone can improve on their efforts and that improvement relies on professional learning and teacher and staff development.

If these conclusions accurately encapsulate the major themes of this chapter, they show that leadership in medium-sized schools is similar and different to that in smaller schools. Person-centred, hands-on leadership by driven and determined heads who see school improvement as a developmental process is one of the main similarities. So, too, are leading by example, an inclusive outlook and low tolerance of poor performance. However, what marks out these heads of medium-sized schools from their peers in smaller ones is the emphasis placed on formal systems and structures, on sharing leadership with the deputy and on the need to create the conditions in the school for everyone to feel involved and part of something bigger than themselves. These heads had to work long, hard and continuously to ensure that there was a sense of unity and wholeness. Organisational cohesion could not be taken for granted, it had to be constructed; thus formal structures were needed and used to a great extent.

It will be seen that there are important nuances and subtle differences between leadership in small and medium-sized schools. Nevertheless, those moving into senior positions in medium-sized schools need to heed the lessons and issues outlined here. Leadership needs to be informal and formal, individual and shared, and about dealing carefully with each and every aspect of the school, but it also involves knowing how these elements fit together and what the 'big picture' of the school looks like. It involves dealing with more people yet still retaining a sense of individuality and respect for individual differences while building a team and promoting a sense of belonging to an undertaking that is bigger and more important than individual interests. Deputies also need to be aware of these dualities and learn to work along these lines. Classroom expertise is an important element of such leadership, but managing and leadership of the organisation are also essential and take on a greater significance than in smaller schools.

4 Leadership in large primary schools

This chapter focuses on leadership and management in large primary schools. It draws upon research conducted into large and very large schools. The chapter begins with an outline of the aims and methods of the research. The next section presents the head teachers' views, looking at what they think it is like to lead a large school, the advantages and disadvantages of large schools, the characteristics of successful leaders, management structures and management development. The third reports on the deputy heads' views, and these largely parallel the issues in the heads' section. These findings are then discussed in the next section, before I set out my conclusions about leading large primary schools.

Aims and methods

The need to study leadership in large primary schools – that is, schools with over 400 pupils on roll – arose from the fact that primary schools are increasing in size, as was noted in Chapter 1. The increases are occurring particularly in terms of large primary schools. To emphasise this point Table 4.1 highlights the increase in number of large primary schools.

The DfES statistics also show that leaders in large primary schools are now responsible for the education of about one in five of all pupils in primary schools.

What is also important about these statistics is the fact that there is now a relatively new group of primary schools emerging. As argued in Chapter 1, whereas once a school with over 400 pupils on roll was considered big, today such schools remain comparatively large; but the biggest schools are now those with over 600 children. The current trend, set out in Table 4.1, shows that there is a new group of *very large* schools developing. Indeed, this group of very large primary schools ($n = 148$ in 2001) are as large or larger than half of all secondary schools. Yet no specific attention has been paid to the particular development needs of the heads and deputies who lead these primary schools.

Having identified this trend I developed a proposal, with Dick Weindling as co-director, to research this group of very large schools (601-plus pupils) and then to compare our findings with those for large primary schools (401-plus pupils). The Esmée Fairbairn Foundation understood the need for the research and generously funded our two-year project.

Table 4.1 Changes in the size of primary and middle-deemed primary schools (1998–2001)

NoR*	Number of schools				
	1998	*1999*	*2000*	*2001*	*Change 1998–2001*
401–500	1,204	1,238	1,256	1,269	65
501–600	245	257	244	255	10
601–700	86	103	109	125	39
701–800	15	13	15	12	−3
801–900	4	7	8	11	7
Over 900	0	0	0	0	
Total	1,554	1,618	1,632	1,672	118

* NoR is the number of full-time pupils only and therefore does not include children attending part-time nurseries attached to the school.

Source: DfES (2002).

The project began with interviews of the heads and deputies in approximately one-third of the very largest primary schools in England, to seek their views on how they have developed, the in-school structures and systems they use to develop themselves and one another, and to identify the characteristics they associated with successful leadership. From the analysis of the interview data, we constructed a questionnaire which was sent to all remaining heads in the largest schools (601-plus pupils) to verify the generalisability of the interview findings and extend our knowledge base. The questionnaire was also dispatched to a random sample of 25 per cent of primary schools with 401–600 pupils to explore how the findings drawn from the very largest schools compared with this group of large primary schools.

The project had five specific objectives:

1   *Characteristics of effective leadership*
    To identify from the heads' and deputies' testimonies the characteristics they associated with effective school leadership in large primary schools
2   *Leadership preparation and development*
    To discover how these heads and deputies had been prepared for leadership and had developed their skills over time
3   *Roles of heads and deputies*
    To discern the respective roles of head teachers and deputy head teachers in large primary schools and to investigate how they worked alongside one another
4   *Compare findings with literature*
    To compare and contrast these findings with the existing literature on effective school leadership

Table 4.2 Details of schools visited

LEA	Number on roll	Total years as head	Head teacher at this school	No of headships
Barnet	600	10	3	2
Ealing	610	20	20	2**
Brent	620	9	9	1
Redbridge	620	12	12	2**
Redbridge	627	6	1	2
Newham	634	16	3	2
Brent	640	15	10	2
Bromley	650	4	4	1
Enfield	654	11	7	2
Birmingham	657	6	6	1
Birmingham	660	15	5	2
Bromley	698	28	20	2
Hillingdon	700	8	2	3
Bracknell	700	17	1	3
Brent	700	14	10	2
Bromley	703	19	13	2
Enfield	714	6	1	2
Newham	720	12	12	2**
Redbridge	733	12	12	2**
Hillingdon	740	18	2	3
Birmingham	750	18	10	2
Ealing	750	15	7	2**
Birmingham	761	11	3	3
Newham	865	12	3	3
Enfield	887	3	3	1
Newham	930	32	5	4

** Previously head of one of the schools on the site before amalgamation

Source: Project data.

5) *Implications for head-teacher development*
   To highlight the implications for aspiring and experienced head teachers, in particular, noting the lessons to be learned about offering appropriate professional development opportunities on and off site to enable them to become and remain successful school leaders and managers.

In the first phase of the research we visited twenty-six schools, spending a day in each one. We interviewed the heads and deputies in each and also toured the sites and classrooms with the heads. The schools ranged in size from 600 to 930 pupils. Details of the schools and the heads are set out in Table 4.2.

We used a semi-structured approach to the interviews which, without exception, we would characterise as being open, conversational and candid.

For the survey a total of 543 questionnaires were sent out to a one in four random sample of the schools with between 401 and 600 pupils and to all the primary schools with over 601 pupils (apart from the twenty-six we had visited). The number of questionnaires returned was 404, giving a very high response rate of 74.4 per cent. The achieved sample consisted of 302 schools with between 340 and 600 (a response rate of 72.6 per cent), and 102 schools over 601 pupils (a response rate of 80.3 per cent). The differential responses between the two groups were not statistically different. The high response means that we can be fairly certain that our findings accurately reflect the views of the majority of head teachers of large and very large primary schools in England.

The fact that some schools had fewer than 400 pupils on roll indicates the fluid nature of pupil statistics. Children move between schools, as all who work in them know; thus pupil numbers fluctuate. Throughout this research we found that all the statistics and tables we used had to be treated as 'provisional' rather than absolute. The same problem also applied in the small-school research and, indeed, applies to all schools.

As anticipated, the overwhelming majority of large primary schools were located in urban areas. Those in mainly urban areas amounted to 87.4 per cent, only 1.7 per cent were in mainly rural areas, while 10.9 per cent had a catchment area that displayed a mix of urban and rural features.

The head teachers' views

Here I shall report what the heads had to say about: leading large primary schools; the advantages and disadvantages of large schools; the characteristics of successful school leadership; management structures; management development.

At one time the majority of head teachers in English primary schools were men. However, the proportion of women heads has gradually increased. According to DfES figures in 1992, 50.6 per cent of heads were men and 49.4 per cent women. By 2002 this had changed to approximately 40 per cent male and 60 per cent female heads. However, out of our sample of 404 head teachers of large primary schools, 56.7 per cent were men and 43.3 per cent were women. It seems that although currently more women than men are heads of primary schools, this pattern is not reflected in larger primary schools, where the heads are still more likely to be male than female. Further analysis of our data showed that the proportion of male or female heads was not significantly different for schools with more or fewer than 600 pupils.

We also collected data on the average number of years individuals had spent as heads, the number of years they had been heads of their present schools and the number of headships they had held. Combining this information we found that men had longer experience of headship than women and had been heads of more schools than women. These findings are in line with the fact that women generally become heads later in life than men and move around for jobs less than men do. Our data also showed that a higher proportion of women were appointed to their first headship in larger schools than men.

Taking the last two points together presents an interesting scenario. Men are more likely to go to smaller schools for their first headship, and, after some success there, move on to larger schools. This pattern has ensured that they have experience of headship in rather more schools than their female counterparts. It may also imply that while some men are more confident than women in applying for headships at an earlier stage in their careers, they are less likely than women to see themselves as ready for a large or very large school. Moreover, we would need to be confident that experience in smaller schools is relevant to headship in larger schools, for the male pattern to be advantageous. If it is not, then the trajectory of (some) women heads may be more suited to preparing them for large headships.

A third of the heads said they had a regular teaching commitment which averaged four hours a week: 36 per cent of the heads of the schools with fewer than 600 pupils said they had a regular teaching commitment, compared with 25 per cent of the heads with more than 600.

Leading large primary schools

Asked what it was like to lead a large school, some of the heads explicitly said how much they enjoyed the role:

> *I love this job.*

> *It is very rewarding. You deal with such a lot of issues, but it does monopolise your life – half-terms and summer holidays go.*

While many of the heads revelled in the role, they acknowledged that the job required a lot of time because in very large schools there was much more to manage, in particular people:

> *Everything you do is so much more time-consuming because there are so many more people.*

> *There are just so many relationships – year groups to one another, different groups of people.*

Therefore:

> *You need to be very organised*

> *The thread which runs through this school is SYSTEMS, formal, clear systems. You cannot rely on informality. It is a primary school, but not informally so.*

One major reason for the need for organisational structures and systems was that the heads realised they had to involve other colleagues and delegate tasks to them because there was just too much management and leadership for a single person to handle. However, not all the heads found 'letting go' (Southworth 1998: 62) easy:

I have kept the day-to-day stuff for me and I try and run it as a smaller school, but I have had to delegate lots – and I have had to learn to do that – I prefer the hands-on approach, but I cannot do as much as I did in my previous school.

Leading a large primary school was seen as stimulating yet also demanding because of having to deal with so many individuals and groups and the need to establish and maintain organisational systems which ensured the school ran smoothly given that no one person was able to provide sufficient 'hands-on' leadership by themself. The following remarks, from a head who had worked in two other schools, neatly summarise the heads' responses:

It is interesting and enjoyable. Issues hinge around size – numbers of pupils, staff and parents. You need very tight systems and structures and good people to manage them, so staff resourcing of systems is important. You cannot control everything, it is not 'my' school, you cannot know everything or everyone – you cannot know the names of every pupil. You have got to delegate, but first make sure you have got people in the team you are confident in. A good deputy is really essential here.

The survey data reinforced these findings and we found there were no significant differences between the schools with 401–600 pupils and those with 601 plus. Briefly summarised, the data reveals that the heads saw the job as: demanding, complex, exciting, very rewarding, very tiring, and stimulating (in that order).

Advantages and disadvantages of leading a large primary school

We wanted to explore with the heads what they saw as the advantages and disadvantages of very large schools. Their answers from the interviews concerning the perceived *advantages* of large schools fell into four sets of related ideas:

1   Lots of staff expertise
2   Many opportunities for peer support
3   Greater financial flexibility
4   Enhanced provision for the pupils.

The heads repeatedly mentioned the fact that having more staff meant an increase in the amount of teacher expertise available in the school:

With a larger staff there is so much more expertise to share.

The large numbers of staff mean there is more talent.

The use and deployment of this expertise took several forms, including:

We have two people leading each curriculum subject.

We have got large teams and staff can cover the whole of the curriculum. We can also create new, imaginative posts such as our curriculum manager post.

Consequently, there was: '*Much more potential for delegation*'.

The fact that there were many colleagues also meant staff had greater opportunities for finding and receiving professional support:

Year groups of staff are very supportive to each other. Lots more opportunities for staff discussion and camaraderie.

The workload of planning can be shared.

Moreover, such support also facilitated professional growth because there was: '*The stimulation of so many colleagues*'. Indeed, professional development was seen as an important advantage. Several heads stressed that there were:

Far more staff development opportunities. Lots more staff sharing.

Expertise – you get a tremendous range of staff expertise and this can pull up staff weaknesses. Year group and phase planning is developmental – it is INSET.

There were also advantages in having relatively larger school budgets. These benefits included:

The budget gives you lots of flexibility and scope.

There are internal promotional opportunities too.

The economies of scale. Music specialist, SENCO, etc. are able to work with children out of class and with booster groups. You cannot do that in a smaller school.

We have lots of different projects running; larger schools are dynamic places.

We tested these ideas out in the survey we conducted. *Tables 4.3 and 4.4* show the percentage of heads who: agreed, disagreed, or did not know. While the last column shows the mean, or average from the five-point scale.

While the surveyed heads agreed with most of the statements, there were mixed views on whether specialist roles enabled large schools to achieve better pupil outcomes. These findings confirm the qualitative data. Four points emerge strongly:

1 There is more staff expertise available in the school.
2 There are many opportunities for peer support for teachers.
3 There is enhanced curricular provision for pupils.
4 There is greater financial flexibility.

Table 4.3 Advantages of large primary schools over smaller ones

Item	Percentages			
	Agree	*Disagree*	*Don't know*	*Mean*
There is much more staff expertise available in the school.	96	3	1	4.46
Many opportunities for peer support for teachers.	99	1	0	4.58
There is enhanced curriculum provision for pupils.	78	12	10	4.06
The specialist roles enable better pupil outcomes.	51	24	25	3.39
There is more financial flexibility.	76	19	5	3.91

Source: Project data.

Turning to the *disadvantages*, the interviewees largely centred on issues of communication. The heads' comments about communication involved four interrelated aspects. First, many heads said they did not know the children as well as they used to when they worked in smaller schools, and in expressing this some conveyed a sense of disappointment or even loss:

> *You cannot know all the children as intimately.*

> *I don't know all the children's names – it is important to me – but I cannot do it.*

Second, some of the heads felt this was not only a communication problem inside the school which influenced head and pupil relations, but was connected to parents' perceptions of large schools:

> *Some parents think their child may get lost in a large primary school.*

This head was also quick to add that when the school was inspected by a team from OFSTED the inspectors said: 'we ran the school like a smaller one'. At other points in the interviews and during the tours of the schools, many of the heads explained how they were trying to ensure that children did not feel overwhelmed by the sheer scale and numbers of people on site. For example, two of them said:

> *You need to get a family feel in a large school.*

> *Ensure it is never a big school, try to create small units which are secure places and spaces.*

Third, some voiced worries about head–staff relations:

> *It is easier for staff to feel left out and under-valued. In a big school you need to spend more time dealing with the staff. You must keep personal contact.*

Staff and children can feel lost. Trying to meet everyone and know everyone is very difficult. We have seventy-five adults in school, plus our part-time tutors.

These statements demonstrate a shared belief in the primacy of personal contact and face-to-face dealings with staff and pupils alike.

Fourth, several of the heads expanded on these concerns, and their comments showed that they were uneasy about the possibility of the school becoming impersonal to staff and pupils alike and that they, as heads, might no longer be in touch with the human side of the school, which for all of them, was the core purpose of their work:

You can become detached. You can lose the 'hands-on' because you cannot get round the school enough (and so there is) not enough contact with the staff. Communication is a big issue and you have to review the procedures constantly.

The fear that people will be anonymous. Big schools need to sustain intimacy and belonging. Big schools require different management styles to avoid becoming impersonal.

Keeping in touch, direct touch with individuals – pupils, staff and the curriculum. You have to work hard at communication.

Sustaining contact and keeping in touch were such imperatives to these heads that they were aware that their approaches to headship had shifted to ensure that these features remained attributes of the organisation, rather than becoming lost as the schools grew in size. The following comment suggests how one head attempted to overcome these disadvantages:

As head you can only control through others, you have to let go – that is a very difficult thing to do. Also, you have to skill-up others to take control. For a primary head that is very hard because as a head in a smaller school you know every child, every member of staff, every parent and they all have access to you. In this school it's impossible. I have no part in some of these things now. So I cannot operate as I used to do. The deputy also has a very different role. You have to delegate a lot, especially to the deputy head.

Our survey results showed the levels of agreement and disagreement shown in Table 4.4.

Furthermore, using the over/under 600 size difference showed that the following items were seen as more of a problem in the largest schools:

- The head cannot know all the children;
- The head's leadership can become more detached;
- Communication within the school is a major challenge.

For all the other items there were no significant differences between the two categories of large and very large schools.

Table 4.4 Disadvantages of large primary schools over smaller ones

Item	Percentages			
	Agree	Disagree	Don't know	Mean
The head cannot know all the children.	60	37	3	3.24
The head's leadership can become more detached.	58	41	1	3.22
It is very hard to sustain the primary school ethos.	15	82	3	2.04
Dangers of the school becoming impersonal.	22	75	3	2.29
Children can be overwhelmed by the size of school.	20	75	5	2.31
Parents are concerned by the size of the school.	12	78	10	2.11
Communication within the school is a major challenge.	59	40	1	3.23

Source: Project data.

The lower means in Table 4.4 showed that the heads were less clear about the disadvantages compared with the advantages of large primary schools. With means of over three, heads tended to agree that they could not know all the children; that internal communication was a major challenge; that the head's leadership could become more detached. The other four items had means below three, which suggested that many heads did not agree that these were disadvantages of large schools.

In terms of the items about sustaining a primary school ethos, the dangers of the school becoming impersonal, children being overwhelmed by the size of the school and parents being concerned about the size of the school, these were not generally supported by the respondents. Although a minority of heads thought these ideas were correct, between 75 per cent and 80 per cent did not. We included them in the questionnaire because some of the interviewees suggested these were dangers, but they were not supported by the quantitative data.

We directly asked the interviewed heads who had worked in small schools to say what differences they had experienced between small and large schools. Three points were made consistently: the importance of communication; delegation; and the need for strong management structures. For example:

> *You delegate more than in smaller schools; you rely so much more on working through others.*

> *There is more delegation. I look to the middle managers to sustain personal contact for me, but it is not always possible with some managers. Training for the middle managers is vital. Much depends on the quality of middle managers and developing a common language, shared understandings, values and beliefs.*

> *The differences are that you delegate far more and you must create small schools within the school, hence we have three phases – early years, which is the nursery and Year R, Years 1, 2 and 3 and years 4, 5, and 6.*

> *The level of delegation (is different). You have to delegate in a large school and be clear about who is doing what. There are about a hundred people to manage here, including all the support staff.*

Therefore one of the big differences between very large and smaller schools was the degree to which leadership was more distributed in larger schools. However, this affected the nature of headship:

> *The head's personal example is diluted, it is not as powerful. It is important for the head to be accessible and approachable although you are more a figurehead.*

As a consequence of high levels of delegation the quality of middle managers and their development needs were mentioned by several of the heads:

> *It is essential to have good phase (middle) managers. Year coordinators play a big role too. There is lots of teamwork too, but it is smaller units, not as a whole school.*

> *Staff do get management experience here. The year coordinators here manage the equivalent of small schools. Middle management is essential, and so too is training.*

Given the need for both delegation and effective communication, the need for sound systems and organisational structures was again highlighted:

> *You have got to set up structures and systems.*

> *You need a good management structure. Communication is the root.*

The results from the questionnaire concerning the heads' perceived differences between large and smaller schools showed that in comparison with smaller schools the main differences were:

1   There is a lot more delegation.
2   You rely far more on phase leaders and middle managers.
3   You must use teams to a far greater extent.
4   An effective SMT is essential.
5   You must use more formal systems of communication.
6   As head you spend a lot of time on site management.

Moreover, the larger the school the more these differences were recognised because when we analysed responses from the schools with 401–600 pupils and those with 601+ pupils there were significant differences in the strength of opinion about these six items.

Characteristics of successful school leaders

When asked to say what were the characteristics of successful school leaders, four main interrelated characteristics were identified by the heads:

•   Working through others
•   Teamwork

- Vision
- Keeping in touch.

Working through others was expressed in terms of delegation, letting go and trust:

> *The number one is real delegation and having the courage to do it.*

> *You have to let go and you must let others take responsibility. There is some risk in this though, because you are then at the mercy of others! But if you do not let go, you will go under.*

> *You have to trust others.*

Teamwork involved team-building and sustaining a sense of organisational cohesion:

> *You have got to build successful teams in all parts of the school and work hard at bringing all the parts together.*

Vision appeared to mean knowing where you and the school were going, ensuring others were prepared to travel in the same direction and maintaining a 'big picture':

> *You need a clear structure and vision. You also need flexibility in a large school; the head cannot do it all. You need to get ideas from others.*

> *You have to be good at the big picture and you have got to understand how things relate to each other. You need a high energy level and a good memory to keep hold of all that is happening. It helps if you have a partner – here it is the deputy because dual leadership matters.*

Keeping in touch was, in part, about communication, but it was also about ensuring that leadership and management were informed by accurate knowledge about what was happening in the school:

> *Keep in touch with what is happening, it is easy to fail to recognise what is happening. You need the ability to think strategically and to translate them into workable, practical systems.*

These four characteristics have much in common with what the heads of small and medium-sized schools said. However, the difference between the heads of larger schools and those of smaller ones is really a matter of degree rather than kind. The heads of large schools repeatedly made these points. For example, working through others, teamwork and keeping in touch are points made in previous subsections in this chapter. Possibly only vision is a new finding here. What is interesting about the notion of vision is that it involved being able to assemble a big picture from many pieces: how the school was performing, where it was going. Fitting together these pieces was part and parcel of vision.

Management structures

The need for management structures and systems has already been highlighted in many of the heads' comments. Yet within this topic lay an important – possibly critical – element, namely the senior management team (SMT). The size, composition and even the title of this body varied considerably across the schools we visited. The smallest consisted of a group of three (e.g. head teacher, deputy and senior teacher), while the largest numbered nineteen people including the head, deputies, assistant head and senior teachers. Several of the schools used a two-tier system so that in addition to the larger SMT there was an 'inner cabinet', 'star chamber' or 'headship team' consisting of the head and deputies who often met informally before school and sometimes more formally once a week. In some schools the senior teachers were also invited to these weekly meetings, but in others the SMT met monthly or three times a term.

The basic structural unit in the very large schools was the year team of three or four teachers plus their classroom assistants. Each team usually had a named leader, although this was not always the case. In addition to this 'horizontal strand', the schools also had the 'vertical' structure of the curriculum, where curriculum managers or subject leaders (the naming of these posts varied from school to school) had whole-school responsibility for their subject area. These horizontal and vertical strands create a matrix model of responsibilities. In some ways this matrix model of management mirrored that commonly found in secondary schools, where subject departments and heads of year form a well-established pattern.

Looking across the schools, it was difficult to find a clear pattern to the roles and titles allocated to the members of the SMT. The most frequent model was a phase structure, where each of the senior staff took responsibility for two year groups, though it was also quite usual to divide the school into Key Stages. In addition, we came across various other combinations, which meant that senior staff might have responsibility for the curriculum and for overseeing some of the year teams. The most unusual structure, found in one case, involved dividing the school into three vertical teams so that each of the three senior staff members had a team of seven teachers (one from each year).

Overall, it seemed that in these very large schools there had been a move away from a school structure strongly based on the curriculum to one that was predominantly based on year groups, phases or Key Stages, with curricular responsibilities occupying a less prominent role in the structure.

About half the heads we visited thought their SMT was very effective. They saw the importance of getting a good balance of youth and experience in the team, and they wanted 'ideas people' not just a group of 'yes-men/-women'.

Table 4.5 Number of senior staff

	Percentage of schools		
Numbers	Deputy heads	Assistant heads	Senior teachers
0	4.2	73.0	50.3
1	83.4	12.9	10.4
2	11.4	10.1	14.1
3	0.7	3.5	10.8
4	–	0.5	8.1
5	0.2	–	4.7
6	–	–	1.5

Source: Project data.

The best teams had complimentary skills, were seen to be hard-working with no negativity or disillusionment, and were respected by the staff as a whole. In all the schools the SMT needed to be seen to speak with one voice in public. As one head said: 'Agree in public, disagree and discuss in private.' Another expressed the same point: 'We work as a cabinet and have collective responsibility.' A third head said: 'Trust is essential. The SMT must be leakproof.'

The survey produced a wealth of data. For example, Table 4.5 shows the numbers of deputies, assistant heads and senior teachers in all the schools we surveyed.

The great majority of surveyed schools had one deputy head. This finding should be compared with secondary schools of similar size, which often have more than one deputy head.

As might be expected, the larger schools had more deputies and assistant heads than smaller ones. However, the average number of senior teachers was *not* significantly different in those schools with over or under 600 pupils on roll.

The use of assistant heads is uneven and difficult to interpret given the shift in terms in the last few years. Whereas some once argued for deputy heads being called assistant heads (Southworth, 1998), now assistant head is a position in its own right indicating the number two deputy. All this means that the position of deputies is even more unclear, while the respective roles and responsibilities of deputies and assistant heads also lack clarity.

Turning to the size of the SMT, Table 4.6 shows the range of staff numbers who were members of the SMT in the surveyed schools.

The mean size of senior management teams across all the schools was 5.25. Schools with fewer than 600 pupils had an average of 5.09 in their SMT compared with 5.73 for those with more than 600; not surprisingly, larger schools had larger SMTs.

This suggests that leadership in large schools is less about heads and deputies working together than about heads, deputies and other senior staff all being involved. Thus it seems that more staff are involved in running the primary

Table 4.6 Size of the senior management team

Number of people	Number of schools	Percentage
2	8	2.0
3	42	10.4
4	91	22.6
5	99	24.6
6	82	20.4
7	49	12.2
8	22	5.5
9	5	1.2
10	1	0.2
12	2	0.5
19	1	0.2

n = 402   Missing data: 2
Source: Project data.

school than was formerly the case. However, it is unclear whether and how SMTs are involved in decision-making, and whether they have an active role or are merely a 'sounding board' for the head.

The survey data also showed that the heads believed:

1 The SMT plays a major role in strategic planning.
2 Senior posts are awarded for organisational rather than curriculum duties.
3 Teachers in most of the year groups work effectively as teams.
4 We have very effective phase/Key Stage leaders.
5 The head and deputy work well as partners.
6 The SMT is highly effective.
7 Phase leaders need specific training for large schools.

Overall, the picture we developed of the management structures was that there was considerable variation across the schools. SMTs were individual in their composition and size, although typically they were composed of between four and six members. Effective SMTs were positive in outlook and presented a united front to the school. A major role played by the SMTs concerned strategic planning. Most schools had just one deputy head, while the number of assistant heads varied.

Leadership development

We explored with the heads how they had developed the necessary skills and knowledge to lead their schools and which aspects of their previous posts had helped them in leading and managing a large school. There was a general belief that what had helped them learn to be a head teacher was first-hand experience. On-the-job learning was the most cited example of development:

I learned a lot in my first headship. I have learned a lot from all my previous heads. You have got to learn from experience – you must learn by doing the job.

Alongside being a head, several cited deputy headship as a learning experience:

I was deputy head with a forward-thinking head – that was a big help.

My five years as a deputy head, working with a head who made me see how to work as a team.

Deputy headship, though – as other studies have found – is not always a positive learning opportunity:

I had two deputy headships but they did not prepare me for here because of the lack of management opportunities. I learned a lot of negative things – I learned what not to do.

Other positive experiences were related either to a widening of awareness of practice in other schools or to developing academic knowledge and understanding. Some had worked on school improvement projects for the LEA, been curricular advisers for the LEA or additional OFSTED inspectors. When asked which courses they had done we were told about MBAs, master's programmes, the OFSTED school self-evaluation course, London Institute courses and the National Professional Qualification for Headship (which only one of these twenty-six heads had taken).

Several of the heads had done the 'Leadership Programme for Serving Heads' (LPSH) course:

I have done the first four days of the LPSH which were very good, but not terribly challenging.

LPSH was not that valuable really.

The LPSH was brilliant. It gave me time to think and helped to draw all the aspects of leadership together.

I did the LPSH last January, it was the best thing I have done. It was excellent. The 360-degree feedback was very helpful and interesting.

I did LPSH – the 360-degree feedback was very interesting. I liked meeting the other heads too, who were very good, and we spent a lot of time together.

The themes from the interviews formed the basis of a set of questionnaire items to examine the heads' views on management development and what they had learned from working with previous heads. Table 4.7 sets out the main findings.

Table 4.7 Management development

Item	Percentages			
	Agree	*Disagree*	*Don't know*	*Mean*
You learn your role as head by doing the job.	88	11	1	4.02
I learned from previous heads:				
a) how to manage the curriculum.	49	49	2	2.97
b) How to lead school improvement.	42	54	4	2.86
c) How to structure the school.	50	45	5	3.04
d) How to work with people.	68	28	4	3.51
e) How to use power and influence.	45	46	9	3.01
f) How to read and understand the school culture.	50	41	9	3.13
Previous heads were positive role models.	67	29	4	3.51
Previous heads were negative role models.	74	19	7	3.71

Source: Project data.

The majority of heads agreed with the notion that you learned the role by doing the job. A majority also agreed that they had learned from their previous heads how to work with people. As other research has shown, the heads they had previously worked with had been both positive and negative role models. Their views on the other items were divided.

These findings suggest that on-the-job learning is highly valued and should be utilised in training. Also, heads need to be fully aware that they are role models for junior staff and that they have an important part to play in staff development.

The views of the deputy heads

During our visits to the twenty-six schools we interviewed thirty-three deputy heads and assistant heads. Most schools had long-serving deputies. The average time in post was seven-and-a-half years. Eight of the twenty-six schools had two deputies and eight schools had the relatively new post of assistant head. As suggested earlier in this chapter, there was no simple relationship between the size of school and the number of deputy and assistant heads' posts.

Asked what was it like to be a deputy in a large school, the response was that it was enjoyable but very hard work:

> *It is really exciting – challenging, rewarding, fun, draining.*

> *Brilliant, I love it. The school is just the right size. Three forms of entry means teams of three across the school with lots of expertise, who can work together and pool things.*

While most of the deputies had no regular teaching commitment, others wanted to maintain some teaching; but the size of the school was seen as a determining factor.

I do a lot of the day-to-day administration. Personally, I think that two days' teaching a week is about right in a three-form entry school. It would not be possible to teach with four forms of entry.

The deputies had a lot of responsibility, which several thought was similar to that of a head in a smaller school.

My job is equal to that of a head in a 250 school.

Being a deputy in a large school, in fact, seemed to put some people off applying for headship. As one deputy explained:

I enjoy it. I have been thinking of headship, but these are much smaller schools, and I think I prefer big schools with lots of variety and lots of people. I would find a small school claustrophobic.

We invited the deputies to say whether they saw any differences from working in smaller schools. The most frequently mentioned point was the importance of delegation in a large school. The second clear message was the importance of good communication, which was seen to be more difficult in a large school. The value of teams in a large school was another point that was commonly made.

The deputies felt that in small schools staff were overloaded, especially with curriculum responsibilities, as there were not enough people to share the workload. This was not the case in their present schools because they thought there was plenty of expertise available in large schools.

The key characteristics of successful leadership which were frequently mentioned by the deputies in very large primary schools were: delegation, good communication systems, and structure:

Clear delegation is essential.

Feedback systems through the organisational structure, so that information flows up the school as well as down.

A number of deputies wanted heads to be good role models and to lead by example. Also important was an effective and productive relationship between the head and the senior staff. In addition, several deputies stressed the importance of vision and a shared understanding by the staff, which was harder to achieve with so many people in a larger school. Linked with this was collective responsibility, so that the school worked together as a whole unit.

The deputies were asked to talk about those aspects of their previous posts which had helped to prepare them for their current one. They cited responsibility for leading a phase, coordinating INSET and special educational needs. They also spoke about how they had learned to delegate, to work with teams of staff and to manage conflict. One of the deputies had been an advisory teacher and found it valuable to meet a large number of heads and deputies. Other events which, in retrospect, had helped the deputies' management development were school amalgamations and OFSTED inspections. In general, being given responsibility, together with a wide range of experience of different curriculum areas, teaching in various phases and different schools, were seen as useful preparation for deputy headship. But several people pointed out that being a deputy was still a steep learning curve.

In terms of professional development and training, many talked about LEA management courses as being very helpful, especially those aimed at deputies. Six deputies had attended part-time management courses provided by various universities. All of these were valued. Six of the deputies had also recently attended OFSTED courses on school self-evaluation with their heads, and most said that they had found them useful.

Each of the deputies and assistant heads were asked if they wanted to become heads. Nineteen said: 'No', while nine said: 'Yes', while the remaining five were not sure. Some of the deputies considered that it was now too late in their careers to think about headship, and a few said they had never wanted it. The reasons which deterred them from applying for headship were:

I don't want that much responsibility. It is lonely at the top.

There is stress from all directions.

The pay differential between the deputy of a large school and that of a head is not enough. It is not financially worth it.

Too far removed from the children.

I have enough fulfilment as deputy of this large school.

I feel I am a good deputy and I will be acting head, but I am unsure whether I would be a good head.

Asked about their professional development needs, the most commonly mentioned one was to do more work on pupil data analysis. They also felt they needed training in ICT and the management of school finances.

The deputies also told us what advice they would give to other deputies. Their responses were most revealing about the role. Several stressed the importance of time management:

Be strict about the use of your time. In a smaller school you can go into classes to help someone. If you do it in large school, you will lose your planning and thinking time – you must protect it.

Developing a good working relationship with the head was also frequently mentioned:

First, be loyal to the head and work with them.

Watch the headteacher – listen, look and observe. Build a partnership with the headteacher – make it work – and keep the trust of the staff. Be an able negotiator and mediator.

A number of deputies emphasised the need to establish yourself with the rest of the staff.

Build up staff relationships (with all staff, both teaching and non-teaching) quickly. Work with someone: and develop partnerships – organisation in large schools is complicated, two of you can avoid errors.

Get into classes; find out what is happening in the school. Work on your credibility – prove yourself. Don't go in determined to change things. Work with the team.

Listen, look and speak very carefully. Don't say 'In my last school we did . . .' Plan carefully. Expect surprises and probing questions.

These comments suggest that deputy headship in very large schools is both similar to and different from deputy headship in other-sized primary schools. The similarities are that they: are dependent upon their heads for role definition and clarity about their responsibilities; work in partnership with the head teacher; need to sustain relations with the staff and the head; need to be able to turn their hand to almost everything. However, the differences are that they: have substantial responsibility; manage staff and teaching on a day-to-day basis far more than their counterparts in smaller schools; teach considerably less than deputies in medium-sized and small schools.

It also seems that the additional responsibilities, higher levels of involvement in managing and leading important aspects of the schools' operations and the higher remuneration, compared to deputy headship and heads posts in smaller schools, make the job one they are reasonably satisfied with, sometimes to the point of not considering applying for a headship elsewhere.

Discussion

This section is organised into a number of subsections which focus on: the significance of school size; school structures; leadership development; and head teachers' influence on teaching and learning. These issues have either emerged in the preceding presentation of the findings or underscore much of the foregoing. All certainly warrant attention and discussion here.

The significance of large school size

Once a school reaches a certain size – probably above 400 pupils – this affects school organisation. It seems that an important point occurs when a school increases from two forms of entry to three because this results in a fundamental change in group dynamics as the year teams change from two to three individuals who are required to work productively together. This was what interviewees told us, and what I believe is implied in the data we collected. When year teams move from two to three or more people, it stimulates a need for year-team leaders and thus the schools move towards a matrix structure and away from a more 'pure' curriculum-based organisational structure.

The heads recognised that the main disadvantages for large schools were: first, that the head cannot know all the children; second, that the head's leadership can become more detached; and that, third, communication within the school is a major challenge. Heads always need to keep these in mind and to develop structures and strategies to minimise potential problems.

School structure

The relationship between school size and structure is most noticeable in terms of communications. All the heads interviewed stressed the importance and the challenge of managing effective communication systems. Daily news letters, briefings, meetings, noticeboards and other mechanisms were described. These were used to ensure staff knew what was happening in the school. They were largely 'formal' systems, and many of the interviewed heads and deputies made it plain that in a large school it was inadvisable to rely on informal communication channels. This finding was validated by the results of the survey, where 85 per cent of the respondents agreed on the need to use more formal systems of communication in large schools compared to smaller ones. Thus the organisation of large schools is, in part, aimed at ensuring effective internal communications.

Most schools had adopted a form of matrix structure to organise the school's management and leadership, based on year teams and subject leaders. In several schools, Key Stage or phase leaders were important middle leaders. It was also clear from the data that there is no ideal structure. The organisational charts we collected were complicated and reflected multiple variables such as school history, salary scales, available personnel and individuals' skills and abilities.

The average size of the SMT was about five members, although the data showed that SMTs were variegated. Nevertheless, the importance of the SMT to the management and leadership of large and very large schools is a clear finding. The SMT is a key component in the organisation of large and very large primary schools. It is highly likely that the success of the school rests, in some measure, on the effectiveness of the SMT.

Leadership and leadership development

The traditional approach to headship in primary schools is that of the head dominating decision-making. Previous research over the last twenty-five years (Coulson 1976; Southworth 1994; Hall and Southworth 1997; Southworth 1998) shows that the prevailing pattern is that of lone leadership, with heads having the first and last say on most things. Moreover, management tasks may have been more shared in the 1990s but leadership may not. Research into deputies certainly points to this conclusion. However, the research reported in this chapter shows a greater willingness on the part of heads to involve others in leadership roles. In short, large and particularly very large primary schools are characterised by shared and distributed leadership.

It is important to draw a distinction between shared and distributed leadership. In many primary schools today, there is evidence of shared leadership. Head and deputy partnerships are the most obvious example of this, with the head sharing leadership and management tasks with the deputy, with whom they work closely. This picture is by no means universal, but neither is it uncommon (see Southworth 1998). As schools increase in size, the incidence of senior management teams appears to increase. Thus shared leadership can extend to the deputy and Key Stage leaders, or one or two subject leaders. However, in large and very large schools reliance on the deputy and one or two assistant heads is no longer enough; other leaders are needed. Year and Key Stage leaders thus become key players. When these individuals begin to 'lead from the middle' – as NCSL refers to such responsibility – the school adopts a more distributed approach to leadership. Shared leadership is confined to the head and up to three others. Distributed leadership embraces many more individuals.

What can be seen in these large and very large schools is the use of distributed leadership. This is not to say that it is effective; rather that I simply wish to acknowledge its presence. If this interpretation is valid, then it also adds to the idea, touched on earlier, relating to school structures. Distributed leadership adds to the complexity of the school as an organisation because now there are many more leaders to 'manage' and to develop. These demands, in turn, may alter the focus of the heads' and deputies' leadership because in the very large schools they may have to attend – more so than in smaller schools – to the development of leadership among a large number of individuals. Indeed, heads of large primary schools may need to be highly effective at 'growing' other leaders, and it may be important to emphasise this by evaluating them not as conventional primary school leaders, but as developers of others.

Much the same applies to the finding that there are high levels of teamwork in large schools. Heads, and other staff – particularly deputies and Key Stage leaders – need to be skilled in managing teams and group dynamics. They should be aware of the responsibility to build teams and sustain them.

The heads' influence on teaching and learning

One-third of the heads claimed to have a 'regular teaching commitment'. Although it is unclear exactly what this means, it is nevertheless a rather surprising finding in that it is higher than we expected. However, while just over a third of heads in the 400–600 sized schools taught, this compares with one-quarter of heads in the largest schools. Thus the overall view that the larger the school, the less likely it is for heads to teach appears to hold true.

The importance placed upon middle leaders and teams shows that heads' success in improving teaching and learning is strongly dependent upon their ability to ensure that they influence others. Heads of large schools need leadership teams – the SMT (deputies, assistant heads and Key Stage leaders) – to exercise influence on the middle managers/leaders (namely the year-group leaders and curriculum leaders) so that their influence and that of the head spread across the school.

In turn, heads need to ensure that all leadership efforts are 'congruent'. The need for clear and consistent messages to be broadcast by the senior leaders is crucial, otherwise confusion, borne out of inconsistent and contradictory messages, may occur. Thus heads should not only develop a number of leaders but also need to create consistency and coherence in the way these senior leaders work with other staff.

Conclusions

Four major conclusions emerge from this research. First, leadership in large and very large schools involves a blend of shared and distributed leadership. It is shared in the sense that heads must work closely and collaboratively with their deputy heads and assistant heads as well as two or three other senior teachers. These sets of four, five or six individuals go to make up the senior management team and we know from our data that groups of this size together constitute 67 per cent of the range of sizes of SMTs. The SMT is formed of the leading players in the school, with the head being something like its director.

Shared leadership

This is common in many primary schools, including those smaller in size than those we studied here. In many schools with 200–400 pupils on roll SMTs and heads typically work in partnership with the deputy and a few senior teachers. However, in large schools, given the size of the staff group and the scale of the responsibilities and tasks (staff development, performance management, curriculum development, monitoring and review, school improvement, etc.), there need to be many other additional leaders. So leadership is extended to year-group leaders, Key Stage and curriculum leaders, if they are not already part of the SMT. Thus leadership is distributed across the school.

Teams working alongside one another

In large and very large schools there are a number of such teams. There are the SMT, the year teams and, sometimes, Key Stage teams or lower- middle- and upper-school teams. Individuals may be members of two or more. They may lead one team and be a member/follower in another. Thus individuals need to be able to be effective leaders and followers, at different times. However, the major issue here is that while in smaller schools teamwork is equally as important as in larger schools, the latter contain several teams.

In medium-sized schools (with 200–350 pupils on roll) there is much talk of developing and sustaining a 'whole school'. Usually this means creating a sense of unity amongst the staff and common purposes and goals. There may be some sub-units in these schools, such as Key Stage teams (formerly infant and junior departments), yet there is also a great deal of time devoted to everyone working together.

In large and very large primary schools, there are many more teams. For one thing, the year-group teams form seven separate ones (Years R-6), and we know from our study that these year teams are a major organisational unit in three- and four-form entry schools. For another, there are likely to be two Key Stage units as well. In all these comprise nine teams. In these circumstances leaders, particularly heads, deputies and assistant heads should insist that not only do staff work well within their teams but that the teams also work well together. Thus, bringing the teams together takes on much greater significance than in smaller schools. In short, leaders need to facilitate teamwork and ensure that *teams work* together.

Greater organisational complexity

It follows from the second point that there is more organisational complexity in large schools compared to smaller ones. This was evident in the emphasis the interviewed heads and deputies placed on structures, teams and communication. The need to ensure everyone knew what was happening, that staff were kept informed and that no one was left out or felt neglected, were issues highlighted by many heads and deputies. The heads were also concerned the school remained a human scale organisation, where individuals felt a sense of belonging and where anonymity was avoided at all costs.

Leadership development

One reason for highlighting complexity here is that it relates to the fourth conclusion, which centres on *leadership development*. There are a number of aspects to this issue. First, heads and deputies need to be able to develop other leaders if they are to create and sustain a distributed model of leadership. Second, they need to be able to support other leaders, particularly in enabling them to ensure the teams they lead are in harmony with all the others in the school. Third, heads and deputies also need to encourage 'horizontal' forms of support so that middle leaders help one another. Fourth, leaders need to be able to manage organisational complexity, teamwork and teams working together. Fifth, leadership traditions and role orthodoxies in medium-sized and small primary schools do not necessarily prepare and develop heads and deputies to do this when they move on to work in large and very large schools.

It seems from these four points that the development needs of heads of large primary schools should be rethought. Rather than leaving them to learn how to lead on their own, or trusting that they will pick it up in post or from their previous posts, a more explicit approach or approaches may be advisable. Here there is value in thinking about internships, mentoring and coaching, both for heads and deputies to 'receive' and for them to be trained in using these techniques to develop others in their schools. They may also benefit from in-service provision which focuses on teamwork and where the whole SMT is involved in the training. In addition, there is a strong case for them being enabled to look at how other schools are organised and for them to discuss school structures and systems with their peers and counterparts in similar-sized schools.

Part 3

Emerging themes and conclusions

5 Learning-centred leadership: influencing what happens in classrooms

Having looked at leadership in small, medium-sized and large primary schools, I now turn to consider how the similarities and differences that exist between them affect certain key aspects of school leadership. In this chapter I shall focus on the most critical issue facing heads and school leaders, namely how they influence what happens inside classrooms. This issue is vital to the success of schools and their leaders, and here I will attempt to unpick how leaders do this, drawing on the research presented in the previous chapters, other related studies and my own reflections on them all.

The nature of leaders' influence and effects

The idea that heads and other school leaders make a difference is now widely accepted by researchers, policymakers and practitioners alike. Today the issue is not so much whether heads and other leaders make a difference as *how* they do so. Consequently researchers have turned their attention to tracing the pathways by which leaders exercise their influence in schools.

Leaders influence others in all kinds of ways. We tend to assume that leaders always have a beneficial effect, but this is not always true. Heads and other leaders can have negative as well as positive effects: rather than motivating colleagues, they can frustrate, antagonise and de-motivate others. Also, because schools are social organisations, and complex ones at that – even 'small' schools are socially complex organisations – the connections that exist among members of a school are many, subtle and dynamic. In other words, it can be overly simple to say that a head teacher always influences what others do; these 'others' may be influencing one another just as much, if not more than the other leaders. Thus it is sometimes difficult to know who is influencing whom, especially since influence is not always a function of organisational hierarchies and restricted to those occupying positions of responsibility. Heads, deputies and subject leaders certainly exercise influence, often because of their formal roles, but influence flows interpersonally and informally as well.

Notwithstanding these obvious difficulties in thinking about influence and effects, researchers have latterly begun to identify some of the ways in which school leaders influence others. Hallinger and Heck (1997, 1999) reviewed in some detail school effectiveness studies and the relationship between principal leadership and pupil achievement. Although largely based on North American research and the roles of school principals, their work has proved insightful and valuable, not least because they have developed a threefold classification of leaders' effects. According to these authors, principals influence what happens in the schools they lead in three different ways.

Direct effects: where the principal's actions influence school outcomes
Mediated effects: where principal actions affect outcomes indirectly through other variables
Reciprocal effects: where the principal affects teachers and teachers affect the principal and through these processes outcomes are affected.

(Hallinger and Heck 1999: 4–5)

Reviewing these three pathways, Hallinger and Heck are critical of the first in so far as it ignores the effects of other in-school variables such as teacher commitment or curricular organisation (p. 5). The lack of attention paid to other factors creates a simplistic view of head teacher effects. Indeed, in my view it may develop a simplistic notion of head teacher causation. That is, some believe there is a one-to-one correspondence between what a head does and the school improving. On occasion this may happen as, for example, where the head has a direct input into teaching. As one of the heads in the small-school study said, 'In this school I represent 25 per cent of the teaching.' Hence it is reasonable to expect that given that she was an effective teacher, her practice would enhance pupil outcomes. But so, too, would the other 75 per cent of the teaching!

Heads do influence and have effects, but this also needs to be seen against a background of other factors. Thus across the three previous chapters the idea of structures and systems (e.g. organisational, curricular, staff development) has been a recurring theme. To focus too strongly on heads may be to underemphasise these other factors, which could be of equal, if not greater, importance than the head's personal influence.

Moreover, singling out head teachers' effects deflects attention from how they might combine different forms of influence. Given that schools are complex social organisations, it seems likely that leaders exert their influence along a number of pathways and that the most influential and successful leaders ensure that these different pathways are explored in ways that are consistent and congruent with one another. This is something I shall explore further in the next chapter.

The idea of mediated effects is derived from the hypothesis that leaders achieve their effects on outcomes through 'indirect paths.' Hallinger and Heck say:

> Leadership practices contribute to the outcomes desired by schools, but the contribution is always mediated by other people, events and organisational factors such as teacher commitment, instructional practices or school

culture. This conceptualisation is consistent with the proposition that leaders achieve their results primarily through other people.

(p. 7)

This idea makes a lot of sense. Heads and other leaders work with and through their colleagues. Leaders are dependent upon others putting into practice the ideas and policies agreed and adopted by the school. Thus leaders sometimes have to persuade or convince colleagues to take on tasks or roles they might not consider otherwise. This is what leadership as a process of social influence is all about.

However, Hallinger and Heck also see leadership as mediated by events and organisational factors. For me this signals the importance of leaders using structures and systems to reinforce their own and the school's goals. It is another way of saying that heads need to use as many ways as possible, either singly or in combination, of influencing others. It also implies that the school's culture has a bearing on leadership.

We have known for some time that a school's culture influences what happens there. Culture is a deeply internalised sense of 'the way we do things around here'; it is a set of shared values and beliefs by which members of a group forge an ordered, rule-bound existence for themselves (see Nias *et al.* 1989: 10–11, Hargreaves 1994). We also know that leaders play an important role in creating, sustaining or destroying cultures.

For example, in the study Nias, Yeomans and I conducted into staff relation-ships in the primary school, which became a study of primary school cultures, we noted how important heads were to the establishment and continuation of a culture of teacher collaboration (Nias *et al.* 1989: 95–123). In other words, their leadership was mediated by the cultures they helped to create.

This relationship with culture also relates to the third type of effect listed above. The reciprocal effects pathway presents heads as 'enacting leadership through a stream of interactions' (Hallinger and Heck 1997: 7) through which they address the salient features of the school, such as pupil outcomes, staff morale or commitment. However, in so doing they adapt to the organisation in which they work and change their thinking and behaviour over time. As Hallinger and Heck argue, this model regards leadership as an 'adaptive process rather than a unitary independent force' and allows for the possibility that 'causal relationships may be multi-directional, change over time and even be non-linear' (p. 8). For example, while heads may be working towards transforming the school, they too, over time, may be influenced by what they encounter. They might be striving towards changing the culture, but the culture might also be changing them. A head who aims for staff to work more closely together may also adopt the staff's ways of celebrating personal achievements, say through the use of praise or other forms of recognition.

Hallinger and Heck conclude that the general pattern of results from research supports the idea that principals/head teachers exercise a measurable – though *indirect* – effect on school effectiveness and pupil achievement (p. 26). Thus heads do have an effect, but much of it is indirect because their leadership goals are mediated by their colleagues. Thus a head may wish to improve the quality of teaching in school and set up all kinds of strategies for achieving this, but they will ultimately have to rely on colleagues changing and enhancing their practice. It is as simple and profound as that.

This thinking about leadership effects is important for a number of reasons. Firstly, it moves us away from a simple, causal view of leadership effects. Secondly, it moves thinking towards a more appropriate model of schools as organisations. The idea of leaders having an indirect influence upon outcomes is consistent with the notion that schools are social organisations in which interpersonal relations are the major feature of their operation. Thirdly, the inclusion of other organisational factors suggests that leaders not only work with people but use other organisational processes and artefacts to support their leadership and use these processes as media for their influence. These media embody the messages successful leaders seek to promote. Fourthly, it follows from the last point that leaders should ensure that there is as much alignment and congruence among all the organisational and leadership processes as possible.

The last-mentioned issue warrants some further elaboration here, although Chapter 6 does this to a much greater extent. Leaders do not merely exercise personal influence; the structures and systems they create and sustain also play a part. For example, a head and deputy may well talk about teaching and learning being important, but if staff meetings never focus on them part of the school's communications system is not embodying this aspiration and may even be undermining it. Likewise if classroom observation processes do not focus on teaching or learning but only on, say, matters of classroom storage and use of equipment, then, again, a valuable opportunity to enact the leaders' goals has been lost. By contrast, where meetings and observations are consistent with the wish to concentrate on learning, then these become mutually reinforcing and strengthen leadership.

It also is important to note that whilst Hallinger and Heck's typology works well in the abstract, the reality is somewhat messier. One particular difficulty I have with these ideas is in discriminating between direct effects and mediated effects. I can accept both models and can appreciate their coexistence, but it becomes difficult to draw a line between some head teachers' actions and others, and defining one set as direct effects and the others as indirect. In practice the two kinds will often blend into each other and so become indistinguishable. The same is probably true of mediated and reciprocal effects: they too are likely to overlap and run together.

The threefold typology is an important tool in thinking about how leaders influence what happens in schools and inside classrooms. I tend to think that leaders use all three ways, but mostly the second – the indirect pathways – because they rely so much on colleagues to enact agreed policies and practices. Moreover, the larger the school the more this is true. Also, the larger the school the more there will be reciprocal effects too, since there will be many more of 'them' to influence 'you'. If the typology is a useful thinking tool, then its applicability needs to be tested, and that is what the next section turns to.

Direct, indirect and reciprocal leadership effects in small schools

My thinking about leadership effects has been greatly enhanced not only by Hallinger and Heck's work but by applying it to what I saw when I researched successful leadership in small schools. Here I want to draw on that work to illustrate the theory and to take from it what I think it means for leaders and leadership in medium-sized and larger primary schools as well.

Applying the framework to the heads of small schools I studied led me to identify six sets of points:

1   All three forms of leaders' effects could be detected from what the heads, teachers and governors said. Teaching heads obviously have some direct effect on their schools because they teach a registration class of pupils as well as other classes from time to time. Those who interacted directly with parents and governors also influenced the school's image, reputation and standing in the community and contributed to increasing pupil numbers, which was often cited by teachers and governors as an indicator of the school's success.

The mediated or indirect effects of the heads were described in many different ways by the respondents. The heads were seen as having influenced the schools' goals, expectations, pedagogic and curricular practices. For those who had been in the school for some time there were also indications that, over time, there had been reciprocal effects. Not only had they influenced the school, but as staff changed, as trust was developed with staff and governors, as circumstances altered, so too had the heads shifted some of their practices. In some cases, for example, as their schools increased in size (i.e. pupil numbers) several had ceased to teach a registration class of pupils full-time or for the greater part of the week, while others, for some part of the school year, were teaching less than formerly. Hence, there are visible and clear signs of all three types operating within the work of these ten heads.

2   Because these were small schools it is reasonable to assume that their heads will have a stronger direct influence than those in larger schools, where mediated effects are more likely to be seen. However, what emerges from the study of successful heads in small schools is the suggestion that not only did they have some direct effect but they were also very active in terms of mediated effects. They were typified by a keen awareness that they were working with and through others. They knew that to change what was happening and to improve the schools they and other leaders had to influence indirectly and with determination, tenacity and a clarity of purpose.

3   What is particularly interesting, then, about these heads is that they appeared to have been very effective in how they *indirectly* influenced pupil outcomes. Perhaps because they worked in close proximity to staff and interacted face to face with most staff with great frequency, they could ensure there was much personal contact. In other words, communication and professional interaction between head and staff were *processual*. Their interactions were characterised as continuous, practical and often occurring in the teachers' workplace – their classroom or teaching area. Even in the short time I was present in their schools I could observe some of this taking place. They used conversation – often very quick and brief snippets of conversation – to make their points, follow up issues and items of concern, suggest ways forward, inform people of decisions just made or outcomes of consultations conducted with external agencies or individuals. There was a steady stream of information, involvements and negotiations being transacted between the head and others; yet within all this activity there was point and purpose too. Moreover, in their contacts with colleagues they were warm, considerate and generous.

Such patterns of interaction connect with Fullan's (1991) ideas about managing change and suggest that these heads were especially able at ensuring that teachers' understandings and subjective meanings about desired changes agreed for the school were constantly being negotiated and developed. As individuals anxious to bring about change in their schools – namely improvements in pupils' learning outcomes and progress – these heads were able to do this because they were adept at managing the process of educational change.

4   While the impact of heads in small schools will include some direct effects as well as reciprocal ones, the ability and disposition of these heads to engage strongly with and act on the mediating factors may, in large part, account for why they were so successful. For example, it was noted in Chapter 2 that these heads were:

- Approachable
- Skilled at talking and listening to staff
- Monitored classrooms, teaching and pupils' learning
- Evaluated pupils' achievements and progress.

Governor and teacher respondents repeatedly made these points to me. Given that the heads applied these skills consistently and continuously, they may have been able – perhaps to an unusually high degree – to bring their influence to bear on those who had to implement and carry out planned changes and desired improvements. Expressed another way, these heads worked directly on the indirect pathways to effectiveness.

5   Of course this interpretation does not by any means paint the whole picture. Their leadership also involved the use of organisational, curricular and staff

development structures and systems to support the work of the staff. Although their personal involvement with staff forms the foreground of their influence, in the background were other mechanisms that reinforced and promoted the work and direction of the school. Hence, the fifth point to make is that the heads did not rely on a single or even a small number of tactics by which they endeavoured to make a difference; they used many different means of influencing practice and enhancing outcomes. Moreover, because they knew implicitly that they relied on others they left little to chance in this area and worked assiduously to maximise their indirect effect.

6   It follows from the last point that these heads, either consciously or unconsciously, did not use these skills and tactics in an ad hoc manner. Rather, they deployed them in a strategic way, somehow knowing that when applied in combination they were more powerful. They also ensured that in their detail these tactics promoted the same values, goals and end results. By coordinating these tactics they probably increased their personal effect and impact within the school.

Therefore it is possible to argue that the small-school study points to a picture of leadership effects whereby these heads' success is to some degree – and possibly a significant degree – attributable to their direct effects but particularly their mediated effects. Also, because the heads *engaged* with the mediating factors, and often in a direct and personal way, they were particularly powerful in making a difference within their schools. The strength, frequency and effectiveness of their encounters with staff made their influence pervasive. Their dealings with staff were regarded as warm, fair and open, and they valued individuals and groups, praised them and worked in teams themselves. In these ways they undoubtedly tempered what might in other circumstances have become oppressive conditions of autocracy. Nevertheless, over time, these heads appeared to be irresistible in terms of moving the schools, directly and indirectly, along paths they, the staff and governors wanted.

Tactics for influencing classroom practice

The threefold typology enables us to see beneath the surface of leaders' influence. In turn, it also helps to highlight the importance of heads' indirect effects. Taken together, the typology and study suggest that heads should orchestrate their indirect tactics to influence colleagues. These findings in turn raise questions about which indirect tactics the heads used.

In Chapter 2 I showed that three tactics stood out from among the respondents' various comments. These were:

1   Modelling;
2   Monitoring;
3   Professional dialogue and discussion.

These three tactics interrelate, and – used wisely – should support each other. They also appear to be the main ways by which heads and other leaders exercise their influence.

Modelling

Modelling is essentially about the power of example. Many leaders try to lead in this way, by ensuring that they do what they say and involving themselves in the life and work of the school in order to show that they are prepared to do whatever is needed to support others, lend a hand or 'get the job done'. One of the heads studied in Chapter 2 mentioned that they tended to 'muck in', which I took to mean that they were willing to do almost anything to help out others and ensure that tasks were completed.

It also seems from the teachers' and governors' comments that what the heads did was noticed by their colleagues. In my experience, teachers watch their head teachers very closely: they watch them to see if their actions match their words – do they 'walk the talk'? Leading by example is the foundation of a leader's credibility, which is why teachers watch their leaders so closely, because through their perceptions they are testing their leaders to see if they can do what they ask of others and thus whether they are reliable or credible.

Teachers are also interested in what their heads do because a leader's behaviour gives the strongest possible signal as to what is important to them. For example, if a head attends to pupils' progress and learning by talking with children, analysing outcome data, observing them in classrooms, consulting with teacher colleagues, identifying pupils' learning needs and, over time, seeing how individuals and groups of children develop, then teachers infer from this that the head is serious about learning and regards it from a number of different angles and in a continuous way. In other words, what leaders pay attention to gets noticed. Moreover, what leaders do not pay attention to also gets noticed. If a head was uninterested in classroom practice then teachers would quickly pick this up. Modelling is thus more than demonstrating what is important. It is a key way of focusing colleagues' attention on what counts most.

Another way of thinking about modelling is to say that it has potency because it appears from what teachers said that when heads and other leaders do lead by example this wins the teachers' support. In short, leading by example is particularly powerful as a form of influence for teachers since leaders' actions speak louder and more convincingly to teachers than leaders' words.

Monitoring

Monitoring the nature and quality of classroom processes and outcomes has become a key task and skill set for school leaders over the last decade. In England, the work of the Office for Standards in Education (OFSTED) has played a central role in promoting the value and importance of knowing what is happening in all classrooms across a school. Monitoring is vital to school self-evaluation.

Sometimes, leaders need to monitor for reasons of accountability. Occasionally, monitoring may be necessary where an individual teacher's performance gives cause for concern. However, the form of monitoring I am focusing on here is essentially a type of teacher and staff development.

If that orientates what I want to say about monitoring, I also need to note that I have less to say about it than about modelling or discussion. That is because monitoring forms a major part of professional dialogue. The two overlap and are interrelated.

As this discussion shows, modelling relates to monitoring in that what heads look at has significance and importance for those with whom the leader works. In this sense the monitoring of classrooms, teaching and pupils' learning has both symbolic and practical value. It has symbolic value in that it shows that the leaders are concerned to look closely at what is going on inside classrooms. It places classrooms at the heart of the school and of school leadership. Few teachers, in my experience, will quibble with that priority, even though they may be cautious about how the process of monitoring is conducted. Monitoring also has practical value because it provides shared experiences for teachers and those who observe them. These shared experiences become the touchstones for conversation and discussion, which is the third tactic.

Discussion

Professional dialogues and discussion are important because they develop shared knowledge, common meanings and deeper understandings about classroom practices for all staff. Opportunities to talk about learning and teaching to an interested listener are vital to professional growth because they allow time for reflection, insight and enquiry into one's practice. When leaders talk with colleagues about their teaching they are providing times for teachers to do all of these things, particularly when they encourage a questioning approach which leads on to an enquiry-based outlook to one's teaching and the children's learning.

I say this with confidence because of parallel research in the United States. Jo and Joseph Blase (1998) conducted survey research into the views of teachers about effective 'instructional leaders', that is leaders who influence teaching and learning in classrooms. These authors draw on Sheppard's (1996) synthesis of the research on instructional leadership behaviours, 'especially those linked to student achievement outcomes' (p. 11). Sheppard itemises the following leadership behaviours as being connected to teachers' professional growth and performance:

- Framing school goals +
- Communicating school goals
- Supervising and evaluating instruction
- Co-ordinating the curriculum
- Monitoring student progress
- Protecting instructional time

- Maintaining high visibility*
- Providing incentives for teachers
- Promoting professional development +*
- Providing incentives for learning.

Key: * = most influential behaviours, elementary school; + = most influential behaviours, high school (Sheppard, 1996, pp. 327, 339)

(Blase and Blase 1998: 11)

Blase and Blase emphasise that promoting teachers' professional development was the most influential instructional leadership practice at both elementary (primary) and high (secondary) school levels (p. 11), but they were also aware that until recently we had little knowledge about the behaviours of effective instructional leaders in schools (p. 11). They therefore conducted a survey of:

> Over 800 teachers working in elementary, middle and high schools in the Southeastern, Midwestern and Northwestern United States. Teachers completed open-ended questionnaires on which they wrote detailed descriptions of principals' positive and negative characteristics and exactly how such characteristics affected them and their performance in the classroom.
>
> (p. 5)

Their findings suggest there are three interrelated aspects to effective instructional leadership behaviour:

- Talking with teachers (conferencing)
- Promoting teachers' professional growth
- Fostering teacher reflection.

These three aspects are tied to three other headteacher behaviours that can have positive or negative effects:

- Being visible – versus interrupting and abandoning
- Praising results – versus criticising
- Extending autonomy – versus maintaining control.

Positive effects were associated with the use of visibility, praise and autonomy, while ineffective principals use abandonment, criticism and control (p. 156).

Conferencing is regarded as lying at the 'heart of instructional supervision':

> Principals who are good instructional leaders develop a deep appreciation for the potential artistry of an instructional conference with a teacher . . . Such principals realise that most teachers expand their teaching range only with carefully designed support and assistance.
>
> (p. 19)

The latter point is important because the Blases believe that some principals assume that most teachers can analyse their own teaching and formulate and act on it to develop their pedagogy (p. 20). Such an assumption is over-optimistic, and many teachers can benefit from formal, explicit support systems such as conferencing.

Conferencing is described as involving knowledge and skill in the following areas:

- Classroom observation and data-gathering methods;
- Teaching methods, skills and repertoires;
- Understanding the relationship between teaching and learning;
- Data analysis;
- Knowing how to make the conference reflective and non-threatening;
- Communication skills (e.g. acknowledging, paraphrasing, summarising, clarifying and elaborating on information);
- Awareness of the stage of development, career state, levels of abstraction and commitment, learning style, concerns about innovation and background of the teacher.

(p. 20)

This list alone suggests that leadership which influences teachers and has positive effects on their classroom behaviours requires high levels of professional skill and knowledge about pedagogy, pupil learning, adult learning and human interaction. These skill and knowledge demands become even more evident when the processes of conferencing are identified. The Blases set out five conference strategies:

- Making suggestions
- Giving feedback
- Modelling
- Using enquiry
- Soliciting advice and opinions.

(pp. 28–43)

Blase and Blase go on to analyse staff development and teacher reflection in similar ways. Staff development includes the study of teaching and learning, support for teacher collaboration, peer coaching, action research and the 'application of the principles of adult growth and development to all phases of the staff development programme' (p. 156). The development of teacher reflection included behaviours such as:

Modelling, classroom observation, dialogue, suggestion and praise. The essence of reflection, as we found, was associated with collegial enquiry, critical thinking and expanding teacher repertoires.

(p. 156)

Four important points emerge from the Blases' study. Firstly, there are strong parallels with the findings and my interpretation of the small-school study, which is all the more valid because I only discovered the Blases' study twelve months after I had completed my enquiry and written up the findings. Secondly, leadership of teaching and learning – or *learning-centred leadership* as I prefer to call it – is complex and demanding. It requires high levels of professional knowledge, skill and understanding which we cannot assume head teachers or other leaders will always possess. As other studies show, developing evidence-informed approaches to leadership, management and school improvement require concomitant developments in leaders' skills in handling data, colleagues (Dudley 1999, Southworth and Conner 1999, Saunders 2000) and teaching and learning (Hill 2001). Thirdly, because this study is based on teachers' perspectives, the findings are especially potent since they provide not only insights into what helps teachers to grow, but also what followers want and find helpful from their leaders. This construction of leadership is based on what teachers say *works for them*. Fourthly, it appears that such leadership needs to be designed as part of the school's organisational structures and processes rather than left to chance. This last point becomes apparent when the Blases conclude their study by arguing for schools to become learning communities (pp. 155–167). In other words, learning-centred leaders use direct and indirect approaches, but structure and organise the indirect ways in a conscious and explicit way. This, you may recall, is very much how the heads in the medium-sized schools operated.

The importance of dialogue and articulation

These two studies into instructional leadership and successful leadership in small schools, separately and together show that at the very heart of educational leadership lies the ability to engage with teachers and to create opportunities for professional discourse. This is not the only tactic needed; there are many other complementary ones, as we have seen, but in among them all sit discussion and dialogue.

Thinking about why this is the case I have developed the following line of reasoning to explain both why and how dialogues and conferencing influence teachers' development and practice. Visiting, say, a teacher in her classroom at the close of the day, as many heads and deputies do, and asking that teacher to talk about what has happened is a deceptively simple yet important thing to do. First of all, it requires the teacher to provide an account to an interested other about some aspect of the day. Such accounts are rarely descriptive; rather, the speaker has to focus on something, select key points and edit the storyline. This usually renders the account into an *analytic description*. Simply by virtue of having to focus and present their version the teacher has to make the account 'make sense' for the listener; thus the talker begins to analyse the key components of the incident. From this they can begin to see more clearly what happened, what may have led to what and whether there were any consequences or outcomes which may now warrant further attention. Thus analytical description becomes reflection and enquiry, especially when the listener probes the description by asking questions, inviting amplification or requesting clarification.

This process of describing what happened is also one of *articulation*. The invitation to talk to someone about part of your day is a chance to make sense of the chosen focus. In talking to someone you make explicit to them and *yourself* what may have been going on. We have all had the experience, I am sure, of finding that having said something to someone you suddenly discovered a new insight you were previously unaware of. It is that moment of discovering: 'I didn't know I knew that, or thought that, or felt that . . .' Articulation does that, it helps all of us to make sense of the many incidents and events in our work and lives. Moreover, teachers we know are involved in a high number of interactions each day. Research suggests something like a thousand interactions per day, or five thousand per week, or two hundred thousand per academic year. That is a great deal of material to process and analyse; it is also a great deal of professional experience from which an individual might learn.

We know teachers and heads value learning on the job. This point was made by the heads in all three studies presented in Chapters 2, 3 and 4. Experiential learning was the way they learned most, if not their favoured learning strategy. However, we cannot assume that all of us always learn from our experiences. Talking to colleagues as outlined here is one way leaders can encourage experiential learning.

Thus articulation is in some ways as much about talking to oneself, as well as to the listener. It is a process which can facilitate self-learning. Some call this transformative learning:

> Transformative learning refers to the process by which we transform our taken-for-granted frames of reference (meaning perspectives, habits of mind, mind-sets) to make them more inclusive, discriminating, open, emotionally capable of change, and reflective so that they may generate beliefs and opinions that will prove more true or justified to guide action. Transformative learning involves participation in a constructive discourse to use the experience of others to assess reasons justifying these assumptions and making an action decision based on the resulting insight.
>
> (Mezirow 2000: 7–8)

Whether the process of articulation leads to transformative learning or not, it supports professional insight and the development of professional knowledge. Indeed, it supports professional knowledge that is explicit, practical and applicable. It is the kind of knowledge teachers value and crave. The irony is that they often do not know they already possess it. What leaders can do is help them discover it, articulate and analyse it, share it with colleagues and apply it in their classrooms.

Knowledge management

Another way of looking at this process of articulation and reflection is to think about it as an exercise in knowledge creation. We know that an important part of professional learning is learning with and from others. We also know that when professionals do this they often create new knowledge.

Knowledge creation in the terms being described here is really the creation of professional *craft knowledge*. Teachers talking to leaders about their day-to-day experiences, classroom events, learning incidents and professional puzzles are exploring and refining their craft knowledge. When they do this with leaders, the leaders can note not only who is professionally learning but who knows what. For the leader the process is also an audit of professional knowledge, be it about pupils' specific learning needs, literacy learning, artistic expression, creative processes, kinaesthetic intelligence or whatever.

To move to becoming what Hargreaves (1998) calls a 'knowledge creating school', school leaders must develop awareness of who knows what and who doesn't know certain things. Conversation does that; it also enables leaders to see who would find it valuable to talk to whom, who might lead a staff meeting or seminar on specific issues. In other words, leaders need to manage the intellectual capital which resides in every staff group. Unless and until individuals' professional knowledge is shared, schools will make only poor use of their collective professional knowledge. Staff groups need to find out what they know, 'not least because they know more than they think' (Hargreaves 1998: 27). And 'they also need to know what they do not know – for that is the area where they must create better professional knowledge' (p. 27).

To do this heads and other leaders need to manage the knowledge which exists in the staff group individually and collectively. The idea of leaders developing professional dialogues and of them requiring teachers to describe, articulate and analyse aspects of their classroom practices is both a learning opportunity for the teachers – since they can individually create new knowledge for themselves – and a time when the leaders can collate who knows what in order to manage this knowledge for the benefit of the whole school's development.

Only when leaders and their colleagues know what they know and make these understandings explicit to themselves and to others can this craft knowledge be transferred and applied by others. Knowledge management for leaders involves finding out who knows what, supporting their articulation of this knowledge and providing arenas for this knowledge to be shared with others, transferred to them and applied in their classrooms. This latter point brings us back to leaders modelling and monitoring.

Leaders themselves need to demonstrate that they are learners and that they are capable of applying their learning to their practice. In the small schools I studied, I believe the heads did this. Indeed, heads of small schools are well placed to do so because they teach so much. Yet while heads can thus model knowledge transfer and application, this is not sufficient: they also need to consider monitoring whether and how colleagues apply knowledge shared with them by their colleagues. We cannot assume that teachers will apply the lessons they learn from their colleagues; they need to know that there will be some follow-up by leaders who wish to see how the ideas are working out in other classrooms across the school.

There is much more to explore around these issues, but in this section I simply wanted to make a connection between professional discourse and knowledge management so that the small steps of talking and listening could be seen in the wider context of knowledge-creating schools.

I also want to reinforce a point made previously on a number of occasions. The means of knowledge creation are also ways of 'working with the grain of the psychology and experience of teachers by ensuring they themselves actively contribute to better professional practices' (Hargreaves 1998: 19). Teachers tend to trust other teachers more than they do researchers or policymakers. The idea of learning with and from teacher colleagues should therefore appeal to them, not least because the knowledge gained will be practical and context-specific – what works in *this* school, with *these* learners. This is critically important knowledge for teachers' daily practice. It needs to be shared and developed as much as possible so that the teaching staff become a combined teaching unit; that is, they are all informed by what each one knows.

Learning-centred leadership

It is now necessary to draw attention to the label I have adopted for this kind of leadership. In America, the notion of 'instructional leadership' is used to describe educational leadership. However, as we have found through our consultations at the National College, that phrase is not popular with school leaders in England. Therefore I coined the idea of *learning-centred* because it seems to me that while such leadership is focused on learning and teaching, we need to move to a stronger emphasis on learning than was previously held. Leaders who talk to teachers and listen to their accounts of what has been taking place recently in their classrooms are able, if required, to inject into the conversation a sense of looking at these events from the learner's perspective. In many schools this is also achieved through tracking pupils, talking with them and canvassing their views as well as through formative assessment and self-assessment procedures. In other words, it is increasingly important and common for leaders to encourage teachers to examine their teaching through the lens of learning as well as through their pedagogic principles, intentions and practices.

Also, it is apparent from the foregoing that such an approach to leadership is equally concerned with professional learning. The whole point of these conversations is to stimulate learning for individuals and then to use the outcomes of such dialogues to develop group learning among the staff which, in turn, can be transferred and applied in classrooms across the entire school. Expressed another way, it is the use of professional talk as a way of making sense of one's own and colleagues' practices in order to then try out these understandings, ideas and refinements in one's own teaching and classrooms. It is not simply talking about practice; it is action-oriented talk intended to transform teaching and learning practices.

Therefore what we have here is a highly sophisticated form of educational leadership which focuses – indeed, concentrates – on the key educational arena, the classroom, and aims to be an educative process for all who participate in such dialogues and knowledge creation.

Influencing what happens in classrooms in medium-sized and larger schools

So far the discussion has centred on leadership in small schools. This is because that study was the genesis for my thinking. However, subsequently I have considered what it means for heads and other leaders in larger-sized schools.

In medium-sized schools, it means similar and different things. What is similar here is that heads will use these approaches but so too will their deputy head partners and other senior and experienced leaders, for example the numeracy and literacy coordinators or members of the school's management leadership teams.

However, as has been already highlighted in this chapter, heads and deputies will also need to ensure that strong school structures and systems are in place to support their leadership processes and the staff's work. Therefore heads and deputies should devote time to establishing these structures and systems and to making sure they are fully implemented, as well as to refining them over time. With more staff to manage, policies will need to be both more carefully developed and implemented so that they form part and parcel of a school's procedures and practices. It is also the case that the larger the school the more leaders will be needed and the more they will need to make use of agreed school structures and systems.

In larger schools, heads, deputies and all members of the SMT will need to adopt the learning-centred approaches, exercise such leadership themselves and use the school's structures and systems as effectively as their medium-sized school counterparts. They will also have to devote even more time and attention to supporting and developing Key Stage, year-group and subject leaders in becoming learning-centred leaders and to sustaining the school's structures and systems.

The shift that takes place between medium- and larger-sized schools is that heads and deputies in the latter may need to do comparatively little of the work themselves but instead devote their energies to ensuring that the school's middle leaders exercise leadership in this fashion. Thus in larger schools a major concern of heads and deputies is the development of learning-centred leadership at other levels. This needs to happen not merely because heads and deputies will have little time available to them to do it themselves, but also because they will need many other leaders to work in these ways in order to have an impact.

There is another way of making the latter point. In schools with fewer than a hundred pupils on roll, heads exercise their influence both directly and indirectly on three or four teacher colleagues. That was the case with about half the heads

I studied in my small-schools research project. However, as a school's pupil roll increases, so too does the number of teachers increase; yet for learning-centred leadership to remain effective it is likely that much the same 'leader-follower ratio' of, say, 1:4 remains as a necessary requirement. As further proof of this, where I visited schools with between a hundred and 150 pupils and five or six teachers it was apparent that heads were working closely with their deputies as co-leaders.

In truth I have no strong evidence to support the validity of this 1:4 figure, but the point I am more anxious to make is that as schools increase in size, the proportion of leadership needs to remain at a similar level. In other words, we need to think about the *density of leadership*. In a small school, heads might be able to exercise leadership single-handedly, although many rely on other leaders too. As the size of a school increases, so too does the number of leaders need to rise. In a large primary school with twenty-five teachers, something like six learning-centred leaders will be required, supported by their head and deputy and/or assistant heads.

The notion of leadership density suggests that heads should aim to ensure a leader–follower ratio. Such an index of leadership also implies that as the number of leaders increases so too does the obligation upon heads to develop learning-centred leadership within their schools.

What this discussion also introduces is the idea that there are three different patterns of leadership

I shall label these personal, shared and distributed:

* **Personal leadership** occurs where the head exercises influence often by themself and largely through necessity, as can be the case in small schools;
* **Shared leadership** is where heads work in partnership with deputies, assistant heads – and as the size of the school increases – other senior teachers;
* **Distributed leadership** is where a school has a number of leaders, as would be expected in large schools. Here Key Stage coordinators, year-group leaders and subject leaders will exercise 'leadership from the middle'.

Of course, distributed leadership can be achieved and is desirable in small and medium-sized schools, although it may not always be realistic for all such schools to achieve. While I certainly do not wish to restrict leadership, the point I am making is that these patterns of leadership are what one might expect to see across schools of different sizes. In small schools it is likely that heads will use their personal leadership to a high degree; in medium-sized schools there will be personal and shared leadership patterns; while in large ones there will be a move to distributed leadership as well.

In drawing this section to a close I also want to stress two other issues. Firstly, what is being described here is a pattern for distributed *leadership*, not just management. It is a pattern in which senior management teams, year group-leaders and subject coordinators exercise leadership in their schools. Leadership I defined earlier as a social influencing process, while learning-centred leadership is a process of influencing teacher colleagues to develop, refine, enhance and transform their teaching and pupils' learning in classrooms. Such leadership is much less about managing subject area equipment, resources and budgets; it is much more to do with focusing on and changing colleagues' professional practice.

Second, as a school's size increases the nature of headship and deputy headship changes. For example, once there are more than eight or nine teachers in a school, head teachers and deputies probably need to ensure there are others capable of exercising learning-centred leadership. Around the fifteen-to-eighteen-teacher group size, middle leadership becomes an important feature of the school's development needs, and that is likely to alter the roles of both the heads' and the deputies/assistant heads. They move from being direct and indirect leaders themselves to being indirect learning-centred leaders for teacher colleagues and *facilitators* of year-group, subject and Key Stage coordinators' learning-centred leadership. The focus of heads' and deputies' leadership moves to that of working directly and indirectly on *leadership development*.

The actual figures remain speculative, but their significance is twofold. Firstly, the importance of the 1:4 ratio is really to stress that learning-centred leadership needs to be exercised by individuals who remain close to the classroom so that they are able to model, monitor and discuss practical, pedagogic issues with colleagues. Secondly, the figures highlight how the nature of headship and deputy headship changes in its emphases and content as the size of the school increases. The larger the school, the more heads need to be developers of leaders.

Conclusions

I have argued that school size does make a difference in respect of the nature and character of primary school leadership and demonstrated that learning-centred leadership influences what goes on in classrooms. This was shown by the research into leadership in small primary schools and also by surveys of teachers in the United States. Both leaders and 'followers' are convinced that such leadership works.

The chapter focused on three dimensions to leadership in primary schools. The first dimension is the one which the book as a whole is addressing: *school size*. I have adopted a threefold categorization of small, medium-sized and large schools. This is plainly unsophisticated but allows simple comparisons to be made between them, even though shades of difference exist within each category.

The second dimension is that of *leadership effects*. While a threefold classification was discussed, one of the three – reciprocal effects – is difficult to gauge and likely to be common to leadership in all schools, regardless of size. Also, the significant differences in leaders' effects appear to be between their direct and mediated effects. Hence I focused on these two, and I now want to say that it seems to me that leaders need to consider them both because they are likely to change – often subtly – as the size of the schools they lead changes when heads and other leaders change schools or when the school they are employed in grows in size.

The third dimension is that of *leadership patterns*. Again, three were presented: personal, shared and distributed. Leaders need to think about these patterns because they reflect the 'density' of leadership in schools. The thesis offered here is not only that the larger the school the more leaders are called for, but also that, regardless of size, the 'density index' of learning-centred leadership needs to remain constant. I suggested – somewhat provocatively and certainly speculatively – that learning-centred leadership needs to work on a ratio of 1:4 in terms of leaders to followers.

These three dimensions now can be arranged to form a 'leadership cube'. The aim of Figure 5.1 is really to introduce the idea that the three dimensions relate to one another.

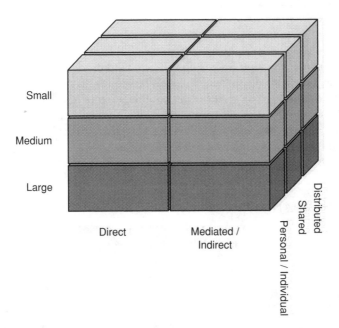

Figure 5.1 Primary school leadership cube: initial model of differential leadership

Given that these three dimensions form such a 'leadership cube', it is now possible to map how leadership is differentially arranged according to the size of the school.

In small schools, leaders – mostly heads – exercise a great deal of direct and a good proportion of indirect influence. Leadership is largely personal, although it does also involve some shared, formal leadership. In some cases it could be distributed too, although this is unlikely to be formally so because the school's budget is unlikely to permit this. The arrangement looks like Figure 5.2.

Small primary schools

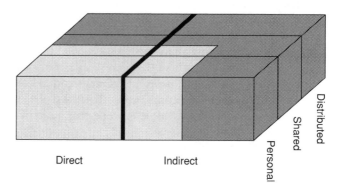

Figure 5.2 Learning-centred leadership in small primary schools
Source: The author.

In medium-sized schools leadership will involve some direct leadership on the part of the head but less so than in small schools; by contrast the amount of indirect leadership will be greater because there are more colleagues to influence. Personal leadership will be exercised, but there also needs to be shared leadership with the deputy, plus a measure of distributed leadership which will grow as the school's size increases. Thus there is likely to be more distributed leadership in a school with 350 children than in a 150-place school (Figure 5.3).

Medium-sized primary schools

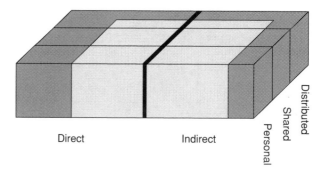

Figure 5.3 Learning-centred leadership in medium-sized primary schools

In large schools, the heads' direct leadership level will be low; their indirect leadership will be high. Personal and shared leadership are present, but there is more distributed leadership than in medium-sized schools. Hence the pattern looks like Figure 5.4.

Large primary schools

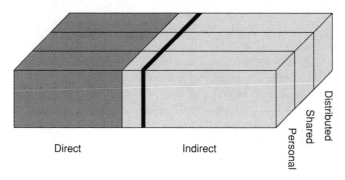

Figure 5.4 Learning-centred leadership in large primary schools

Figures 5.2–5.4 are, of course, ideal types, but I believe they serve to show how the configuration of leadership differs across schools of different sizes. Again it is important to stress that this is a map of learning-centred leadership; other forms of leadership, such as strategic and transformational, may take on other patterns. It should also be noted that the relationship of these different patterns to the use of organisational and curricular structures and systems is constant as these always need to be in place in any school.

However, these patterns are most valuable in terms of raising a key question for all school leaders: 'What is the arrangement of learning-centred leadership like in your school?'

More than anything that is the key issue to address in the light of this chapter's analysis.

To sum up, then, leadership which makes a difference to a school's growth and development is learning-centred. Such leadership uses a blend of direct and mediated forms of influence because leaders can directly guide teaching and learning but mostly they work with and through colleagues and so exert indirect influence on classroom outcomes. Direct and indirect influence flow from leaders using three particular tactics: leading by example, monitoring classroom practice and professional discourse. Professional dialogues involve leaders taking a constant interest in classroom processes, especially pupils' learning, their progress and how pedagogy serves children's learning needs. During these discussions with colleagues, leaders can identify individual and team strengths and areas for development. The process enables leaders to audit who knows what, which in turn allows leaders to manage the development of the school's intellectual capital and thus enhance the quality of teachers' craft knowledge. Thus learning-centred leadership involves working on two levels simultaneously: focusing on pupils' learning and orchestrating teachers' professional learning.

Leaders also need to reinforce their influence through organisational, curricular and staff development structures and systems. These provide clear and explicit procedures which when adopted and used by staff sustain common understandings as well as being vehicles for leadership.

As the size of the school increases there is a need for more leaders to exercise learning-centred leadership. Although heads of small schools can make a difference through their individual efforts, shared leadership is preferable. In larger schools, shared and distributed leadership become imperative because there is value in sustaining the density of leadership across all sizes of schools. In other words, it is important to keep the ratio of leaders to 'followers' low so that each and every leader has a realistic chance of impacting on practice.

However, as the number of leaders in a school increases, the role of heads and subsequently of deputies, shifts from them exercising influence on classrooms to them having some impact on classrooms but also enabling others to develop and operate as learning-centred leaders. When this happens, leaders take on a third level of leadership: that of developing other leaders. In addition to being pupil-and-staff-learning-focused these heads and deputies become leadership-learning-centred as well.

The shifts in the focus and processes of leadership – particularly headship and, to some degree, deputy headship – which occur as the size of the school increases involve a dynamic relationship between direct and indirect effects and personal, shared and distributed forms of leadership. These shifts, which are somewhat contingent upon the size of the school, are not bound by hard and fast rules concerning the number of teachers. I speculated that a ratio of one leader to four teachers might be an approximate 'rule of thumb'. Thus once schools move beyond staff groups of eight teachers, learning-centred leadership needs to involve more than the head and deputy, although this could possibly take place earlier. Therefore, as heads, deputies and other leaders move into larger schools they may need to consider how the size of the school will have implications for their leadership and that of their colleagues, as well as for their roles in developing leaders in these schools.

6 Structures and systems in schools

This chapter focuses on the relationship between leadership, school structures and systems and school size. It is organised into five sections. In the first I explain the significance of structures and systems for primary school leadership. The second section reviews what the heads of small, medium-sized and large schools said and identifies which structures appear to matter more than others. The third shows how systems and structures relate and interrelate with teacher cultures, while the fourth argues that particular kinds of teacher cultures nurture teacher growth. The fifth section then brings much of the discussion together in order to advance the idea of learning and teaching schools and to hypothesize how these might develop over time. The chapter closes with a summary of major issues and my conclusions.

Significance of school structures and systems

Emerging from the three studies reported in Chapters 2, 3 and 4 is the idea that leadership involves the creation and deployment of organizational, curricular and staff development structures and systems. This finding is one which is rather muted – if not absent – in much of the earlier research into leadership in primary schools. Previous research has tended to focus on leaders as individuals and emphasized their role and personal characteristics. The studies upon which this book is based also took these into account because they are important aspects of leadership; however, in the past too much attention may have been devoted to them. Possibly we have dwelt too much on the notion of the leader as a person at the expense of examining other processes and organizational features.

The twentieth-century view of leadership often revolved around a strong belief in the power of the individual leader. This 'heroic' view was based upon a 'belief in the power of one' (Gronn 2000). Such a view may have exaggerated the influence of the lone leader. In many ways this is the same argument used by Hallinger and Heck (1999), which I discussed in the previous chapter. These authors were critical of studies which only took account of leaders' direct actions because these tend to screen out other influential background factors such as teacher commitment, curricular organization and opportunities for staff development.

Indeed, to focus solely on the individual leader may only serve to promote the idea that leadership is all about charisma, and I have reservations about charismatic leadership. It is too simplistic a notion and, often, much too egocentric. Moreover, there is some evidence which now suggests that highly successful leaders are not egocentric or 'celebrity' leaders but self-effacing and resolute (Collins 2001). It appears from Collins's study that it is not the 'larger-than-life saviours with big personalities' which transform companies; rather, it is leaders who are modest and wilful who matter most (p. 20). By 'wilful' Collins means leaders who demonstrate an unwavering resolve and do what must be done to produce long-term results, no matter how difficult this may be. Such leaders perform their duties with 'quiet, calm determination' and rely 'principally on inspired standards, not inspiring charisma to motivate' (p. 36).

Some of that self-effacement and quiet calm was evident in the analysis of leadership in medium-sized schools. Indeed, a characteristic of most of the heads and deputies in all the studied schools, regardless of school size, was that they were modest, quiet individuals as opposed to noisy people forever drawing attention to themselves. This view is also supported by a small-scale study undertaken by a research associate at the National College for School Leadership in England. Woods (2002) found that one of the characteristics of the heads who maintained their enthusiasm for headship over many years was that they were modest individuals.

Yet, despite a growing body of evidence suggesting that many successful heads are quiet and calm leaders as opposed to noisy, 'Look at me' leaders, such quietude should not be confused with a lack of resolve. What distinguishes these impressive school leaders from others is that they succeed in combining modesty with determination. Such individuals, as was noted in Chapter 3, do not want either their schools or themselves to fail in any way whatsoever.

At the same time, though, what could also be seen was how the heads had established and made use of an array of school structures and systems which supported and complemented their individual efforts. Furthermore, this finding was common to all sizes of schools. The only variation was that the larger the school, the more important the structures and systems became.

Therefore the first point of significance about structures and systems is the fact that they soften the focus on 'the leader' and their individual influence. Structures and systems bring into the leadership equation other factors such as staff development, the organization of the curriculum, other posts of responsibility, leadership capacity and density in the school, the work of senior management teams, teamwork and so on. Structures and systems matter because they show that leaders need to create a range of organizational conditions and capacities which work in combination with a head's leadership and management. In other words, structures and systems both reduce attention on the leader and increase the emphasis on the need to establish and sustain an organizational environment for leadership.

Secondly, school structures and systems play an important role in ensuring there is consistency of practice across the school. It has been evident for a quarter of a century that schools can be more than the sum of their parts. While once it was common for individual teachers 'to do their own thing' and operate independently of one another, today this is no longer an accepted way of working. We know from the school effectiveness research of twenty years ago that consistency in teacher approach is important. Studies have shown that where all teachers follow guidelines in the same way the impact on pupil progress is positive. Where there is variation between teachers in their usage of guidelines this has a negative effect (Mortimore *et al.* 1989: 251). The principal issue here is the need to establish unity of approach.

Some have conflated the need for unity as meaning uniformity. I do not see it that way. Common ground rules for how teachers operate are important because they can ensure that, for example, matters of classroom and behaviour management within classrooms and across the school are consistent. Such consistency makes sense, particularly to and for the pupils. A popular cry from children, especially in Key Stage 2, is that some decisions are seen as 'unfair'. In my experience, unfairness often means inconsistency and contradictory behaviour on the part of teachers. Moreover, we know from studies into pupils' perceptions that schools that lack common policies and practices make little or no sense to the children. A school in which there is no consistency is perceived by the students as a kind of organised anarchy where they are obliged to discover for themselves what each and every teacher will and will not tolerate. In such circumstances pupils devote much of their valuable learning time figuring out how to survive with this adult as opposed to the previous one because each successive teacher has their own rules and procedures. In such cases it is easy for children to fall foul of one teacher for doing what another has condoned or encouraged! An effective school is not one which is loosely coupled. Expressed in another way, an effective school is not simply a bunch of high-performing teachers held together by a common heating and lighting system. Structures and systems play a large part in creating the conditions required for consistent approaches and for avoiding the negative effects of teachers working in isolation.

Thirdly, structures and systems are both products and processes. They are products in that they need to be created, or produced. Leaders need to design and develop them, in the light of their schools' situations and contexts. Policies need to be prepared, discussed and, where possible, agreed or accepted. However, they should not become artefacts that are not used; they should be adopted and implemented by all staff. They are not ends in themselves but means to other ends, namely improving and sustaining the quality of learning and teaching in the school. This is why they should be thought of as processes which all members of staff use and adhere to.

Fourthly, seen as processes they become pathways for leadership. They are vehicles for influencing others. For example, monitoring is an important process for encouraging colleagues to learn from one another's practice. It is also a means for leaders to develop colleagues' practice, to audit who is doing well and to identify colleagues' strengths and development needs. At the same time, when leaders monitor what is happening in classrooms they are modelling the centrality of teaching and learning to their colleagues. It is in these ways that leaders lead by example. They show that the structures and systems the school has are to be used actively. In a small school it is the head who needs to do this. In a medium-sized school the head, deputy and sometimes other leaders should ensure they are seen to be using the school's structures and systems. In a large or very large school, the SMT and middle leaders should also model using the policies, structures and systems. School structures are not, as once thought, 'background' factors to leadership; they are part and parcel of it.

Which school structures and systems matter?

This is an important question to raise because if structures matter, we need to be clear as to which ones matter most. Fortunately, the three studies reviewed in Chapters 2, 3 and 4 cast some light on this issue.

The small-schools study included a list of structures and systems which the heads identified when they spoke about influencing what happened in classrooms and how they had improved the schools they were leading. The list is shown again, below:

- School improvement planning
- Target-setting
- Analyses of pupil learning data
- Evaluation of pupil, cohort, Key Stage and school performance levels
- Policies for learning and teaching
- Curriculum policies
- Assessment and marking policies
- Monitoring
- Weekly planning by teachers using learning objectives
- Staff meetings
- Subject leaders' roles.

These items are important because they show that structures and systems are important in small schools as well as in larger ones. To return to a point raised in the previous section, leadership is less and less about how the lone leader influences through the power of their personality or charisma and more about how they lead effectively through a range of strategies and tactics. Expressed in another way, the technology of leadership is not dependent solely on personality; it also rests on organizational conditions and capacities which can be designed, developed and implemented. The list here sketches the outlines of some of those organizational conditions.

It was the HELP study (see Chapter 3), which concentrated on leadership in medium-sized schools, that produced a more detailed analysis of school structures and systems. Appendix 2 presents examples of four schools' approaches. The value of these four examples lies as much in the differences they reveal as in the features they have in common. It seems to me that they differ because they

Table 6.1 Key structures and systems in schools

Use of staff	Planning
Senior management team	School development plan
Clear roles, responsibilities and decision-making powers	Short, medium and long-term plans – planning horizons specified
Job descriptions	Staff development plans
Staff handbooks	Subject audits and targets
Deployment of support staff	Targets for classes, individuals, groups
Rotation and movement of staff between year groups	Teachers plan lessons and teaching collaboratively
Release time	Plans submitted to others/shared
Monitoring	**Use of evidence/data**
Monitor teachers' plans	Pupil self-evaluation
Classroom observation by peers and leaders	Pupil-tracking
Performance management	Benchmarking
Year-group leaders monitor schemes of work and targets	Assessment data collected, collated, analysed, reported and acted on
Budgets and allocations	
Use of meetings	**Training**
Professional development interviews	Staff development plan
Performance management interviews	Investors in People (IIP)
Staff meetings	Staff as trainers
Management meetings	INSET evaluated
Governor and parents	
Support staff meetings	
Planning meets	

Source: Project data.

reflect school contexts as well as individual heads' preferences and emphases. It is important that each school's structures should be tailored and fine-tuned to its individual circumstances, stage of development and levels of performance.

Notwithstanding the need for differentiation, there are also some elements common to all four examples and to the other lists the heads produced as part of the HELP study. These elements are presented in Table 6.1, under the six headings used by the heads to categorise their individual reports.

This second list begins to add more detail to that formulated from the statements of the heads of small schools. There is greater range and diversity, especially when the descriptions in Appendix 2 are studied closely.

This second list also shows just how complex the process of managing a school as an organization has become. The array of issues and topics that leaders are now required to be familiar with and understand has increased considerably in recent times, compared with, say, twenty years ago. Thus one implication which needs to be highlighted is that leaders need a breadth of knowledge over and above their awareness of classroom dynamics and the processes involved in learning and teaching.

Several of the items here overlap and interrelate with one another. In compiling this list I tried to avoid repetition but did not succeed because some items appear more than once. I allowed myself this leeway because I felt it was important to show some overlaps. Indeed, what follows from this feature is the need for leaders to recognize linkages between the items and for them to exploit these connections so that one process may serve to meet multiple goals.

Certain key systems and structures begin to emerge from these two lists. For me they are:

- Monitoring classrooms (which includes providing effective feedback)
- Planning processes
- Communication systems – especially meetings
- Using pupil learning data
- Clear roles
- Target-setting
- Policies for learning and teaching, although policies for assessment and marking pupils' work are increasingly becoming important too.

What this list highlights is a difference between small, medium- and large sized schools. Senior management teams are emphasized in this list but not mentioned at all in that for small schools. Clearly, this is where size does make a difference. In small schools, including those with less than one form of entry, SMTs are rare. In small and medium-sized schools they are unlikely to be significant because heads and deputies working together form pairs of senior managers and leaders. However, at the upper level of medium-sized schools and certainly in large and very large schools the SMT becomes a key organizational unit. This finding from the large-schools research is an important one not least because it notes a development which has occurred in the past decade or so.

However, beyond that general point, little else can be said with confidence about senior management teams. It seems that on average they are composed of five members. In the great majority of schools we surveyed they had between four and six members, although there were exceptions. Also, it appears that membership of the SMT generally comprises the head, deputy head, assistant head and Key Stage or phase leaders. As such the team consists largely of individuals with organizational responsibilities as opposed to curricular roles, though inevitably the two sometimes overlap. This pattern further supports the idea – presented in Chapter 4 – that in large schools leading and managing the organization prevails over curricular concerns, at least in terms of seniority of posts and roles.

If, then, it is true that SMTs emerge as a major structural feature of large and very large primary schools, it is likely that they warrant further examination. The large-schools study did not set out to explore them in detail, and what information there was on them proved rather confusing and unclear. However, Wallace and Huckman's (1999) research into SMTs in primary schools has yielded some important results. They focused on the relationship between SMT and the head, on that between the SMT and the rest of the staff and on the nature of effective SMTs. While their study contains many interesting insights, more research clearly needs to be done. Here I have in mind the need to investigate what impact the SMT has on the school in terms of its performance levels. Also, given the case for more distributed leadership in large and very large schools – which I argued for in Chapter 5 under the banner of ensuring leadership density – we need to consider whether senior management teams are senior *leadership* teams or not, or else a mixture of the two. It may also be useful to examine whether such teams are valuable training grounds for prospective heads and deputies. Do they provide positive professional leadership-learning opportunities? Do they encourage staff to seek out deputy headships and headships?

Returning to the more general issue of structures and systems, we can now say two things. Firstly, organizational, curricular and staff development structures and systems are important. Secondly, we now have a clearer sense of what these actually are. While more detailed and focused work is needed in order to validate or disprove some of my speculations here, their significance as ways of bolstering leadership should not be underestimated.

School structures, systems and culture

So far I have argued that structures and systems are important because they:

- Reduce the focus on 'the leader'
- Increase attention on creating the organizational conditions for leadership across the school
- Promote consistency of classroom practice among teachers.
- I have also speculated that some systems are especially important: structures and systems matter, but some matter more than others.

These four reasons for stressing school structures and organizational systems are strong ones, but there is another one to add. Structures also play an important part in creating the culture of the school. This fact has long been recognized by researchers and practitioners alike. For example, the primary school staff relationship (PSSR) research project I worked on demonstrated that in order to understand primary schools as organizations of adults one must first analyse their formal and informal structures and the ways in which these are maintained (Nias *et al.* 1989).

In the PSSR project we found that a number of formal and informal organizational arrangements enabled staff to work together. Meetings and opportunities for joint planning were two obvious ways of developing professional interaction (p. 34). So too were such rituals and ceremonies as staff gathering for coffee before school started, daily briefings, the celebration of individuals' birthdays and school assemblies which brought the whole school together. Such events increased staff involvement and encouraged individuals to participate, be aware of others, keep in touch with one another and interact positively.

These seemingly low-key events were also important antidotes to the individualized nature of the class teaching system which is such a feature of primary education. Teachers tend to work in isolation from one another. Although there are many other adults in schools today, teachers generally teach a group of pupils by themselves. Where teachers have few or no opportunities to interact socially and professionally with their peers, teaching becomes an independent activity. Each classroom becomes an island and each teacher isolated, either physically or psychologically, from their colleagues. The PSSR study showed that to counteract these tendencies leaders had set up compensating measures enabling their schools to have collaborative cultures as opposed to cultures of individualism.

The study also showed that leaders need to value both individuals and teams. We noted that heads, deputies and other leaders acknowledged the efforts of each and every member of staff, while also recognising and praising the endeavours of teams (p. 60). The latter point was important because it signalled the need for interdependence as well as individual effort. Valuing teamwork increased awareness of shared responsibility for a common task.

The PSSR project identified how a culture of collaboration was socially constructed and maintained in English primary schools. In describing such a culture we noted that it enabled a sense of security to flourish. Security was important because it is a necessary condition for the growth of openness (p. 65). Moreover, a collaborative culture created the kind of environment which enabled a strong sense of trust between individuals to develop (p. 72). When trust was present in the schools it was also clear that the concomitant mutual support and encouragement, alongside security and openness, created organizational resilience – that is, the capacity to cope with exceptional events with few signs of strain – while interdependence created overlapping roles and responsibilities which encouraged adaptability, flexibility and collective strength.

Latterly, the importance of trust in organizations has been highlighted because of its relationship to the creation of 'social capital' (Hargreaves 2001). According to Hargreaves, social capital can be defined in terms of its cultural and structural components. The cultural part centres on the level of trust between individuals and groups. The structural part concerns the networks in which people chose to work. A school 'rich in social capital enjoys high levels of trust which, in turn, generate strong networks and collaborative relations among its members and stakeholders' (p. 490).

These ideas are interesting because they suggest that culture and structure are interrelated. Collaborative cultures create healthy network structures, while vigorous structures sustain collaboration. The relationship between the culture on the one hand and structures and systems on the other is an iterative one.

Collaborative cultures characterized by high levels of trust and interaction – collegial networks – are now recognized by many researchers as important features of effective schools (e.g. Rosenholtz 1989; Fullan and Hargreaves 1992; Leithwood *et al.* 1998). However, the reason for this view is not so much that collaboration and networking are good things in themselves but that they produce and support valuable outcomes. Collaboration generally brings with it opportunities for staff to learn with and from one another. Rosenholtz (1989) best summed this up when she discovered that schools where staff did not interact with one another professionally were 'learning impoverished' organizations. By contrast, those where staff shared ideas, talked openly, planned together and supported one another were 'learning enriched' places.

Collaborative cultures in which staff are able to talk openly, feel secure enough to share their professional concerns and to seek help and advice from one another are environments where teachers are more open, unlike more 'closed' workplaces. It also the case that in such schools 'many (indeed, all) teachers are leaders' (Fullan and Hargreaves 1992: 70). Yet the real power of such workplaces is that they facilitate and nurture professional learning among the staff. Collaborative cultures make schools better places for teachers to work in, which is important; but even more so is the fact that they enable teachers to grow and develop as teachers.

Learning primary schools

Schools as organizations are changing. Despite their nineteenth-century designs and architecture and their twentieth-century assumptions about organization and instruction, there are signs that many leaders and staff members are striving to transform them. While little can be easily done to alter the physical structure of the buildings, many leaders are redesigning the social and learning architectures within their schools. Moreover, much of this redesign process aims to alter the school as a professional learning environment for teachers.

Over the course of a series of related studies I personally conducted or was involved in as a team member during the 1990s, I came to appreciate that what underscored many schools' success was the way the school as a workplace was also a workshop for teacher and staff learning. In a study which followed on from the PSSR project, which examined whole-school curriculum development – or WSCD for short (Nias *et al.* 1992) – the project team saw how professional learning was a central feature to the school's development of the curriculum. The research reported on how in each of the schools a dual approach was under way in which the professional development of individual teachers was balanced with the growth among them of a sense of educational community. Furthermore, leadership was an important factor in managing both of these processes and in sustaining the balance between them. Leadership was most obvious in terms of the actions of head teachers, but deputy heads and subject leaders also played important roles.

The significance of the WSCD project was twofold. Firstly, it highlighted the fact that teachers' professional learning lies at the heart of school improvement. Secondly, it was able to connect staff learning to teacher cultures. The project showed that:

> The key ingredient for school development is teacher learning. We now believe that the existence of a collaborative culture is a necessary condition for whole school development because it creates trust, security and openness. Yet, these are not sufficient conditions for growth. For growth to take place, at the level of either the individual or the school, teachers must also be constantly learning. The challenge for staff in primary schools then, and for those who support them, is to establish a culture which facilitates teacher collaboration whilst, at the same time, enabling teachers to learn from each other and from courses outside the school. The presence of both these factors will enable professional debate and challenge to occur in a climate of trust and openness, thereby ensuring that all the risks and discomforts of learning are counterbalanced by mutual support and a concern for individuals.
>
> (Nias *et al.* 1992: 247–248)

In short, work-based learning was shown to be a vital ingredient in how primary schools learn.

This finding was also borne out by the Improving the Quality of Education for All (IQEA) project. This school improvement project was committed to an approach to educational change that focused on pupils' achievements and to strengthening the schools' capacity to cope with change. Over time we identified six interrelated internal conditions or processes which increased schools' capacities to improve:

1   Enquiry and reflection
2   Collaborative planning
3   Staff, pupil and community involvement
4   Staff development
5   Coordination strategies
6   Leadership.

(Ainscow *et al.* 1994: 11).

These process conditions supplement the ideas developed in the previous two (PSSR and WSCD) projects. They include professional learning, but within a framework of prioritising and planning of improvement efforts at the school level. They emphasise that improvement has to be managed and led and that monitoring and evaluation of the school's work have a part to play in the enterprise. Nor should it be overlooked that these six conditions imply that a particular type of teacher culture needs to exist or to be developing in schools if they wish to enhance the quality of pupils' learning. The culture which these conditions imply is one characterized by teacher interaction, professional discussion, school-based professional development and joint work – in a phrase, a collaborative culture.

These ideas led to a fourth project, the Essex Primary School Improvement (EPSI) Research and Development programme. This programme, conducted in partnership with Essex LEA advisory and school improvement staff, studied how teachers in the twenty-two participating primary schools worked towards improving the quality of teaching and the pupils' learning. The EPSI project acknowledged that school improvement is essentially about self-improving schools, aided, from time to time, by external support. It encouraged a data-driven, evidence-informed approach to school improvement including the analysis of performance data, action planning and target-setting and promoted the notion of teachers-as-researchers through the use in schools of enquiry, reflection and evaluation.

The main findings were, firstly, that a clear and sustained focus about what the school was tackling was a vital ingredient in improving schools. Secondly, establishing a focus and checking progress towards it required a variety of systems and processes to be put in place in the schools. These systems were those associated with school self-evaluation namely auditing, monitoring and data analysis (Southworth and Lincoln 1999: 203).

These findings led to the conclusion that school self-evaluation was not only central to the process of school improvement but the very basis of all change efforts. School self-evaluation, as advocated by OFSTED (1996, 1998), the DfEE (1997) and which is the core curriculum of the National College's 'Headfirst' programme, plays a significant role in enhancing primary schools' levels of performance. However, this approach is itself further enhanced when there is active leadership from head teachers and when they develop shared leadership by involving deputy heads and senior teachers. Linked to leadership is the fact that developing self-evaluation in schools and using an evidence-informed approach to improvement requires the teacher culture in many schools to change. New or stronger workplace norms are needed which enable (as opposed to disable) peer analysis, classroom observation, feedback, collegial challenge and frank discussion about performance and pupil progress without staff becoming defensive or moving into denial. Self-evaluation is further strengthened when pupils' perceptions about their learning and schooling are included. The EPSI programme demonstrated the value of asking pupils about their experiences of school, and these perceptions, in turn, informed, shaped and energised the process of school improvement in several of the participating schools in a powerful way.

Another project I conducted, which reinforced all of the foregoing was an evaluation of primary school improvement in Birmingham LEA. However, the Birmingham project placed a higher emphasis on staff planning 'intensive interventions'. Teachers' *targeted actions* in classrooms led to improvements in the quality of teaching and to pupils' learning (see Southworth 2000). Staff took as their starting point pupils' achievements and looked at how these could be improved by addressing identified learning needs. They did not, therefore, begin school improvement from outside the classroom and, somehow, try to work towards classroom improvements; rather, they were steadfastly classroom-focused. Moreover, they focused on changing their teaching in order to serve the children's identified learning needs better.

Taken together, these studies suggest that there is a high degree of correspondence between teacher and staff development practices on the one hand and the institution's capacity to grow and improve on the other. One of the links between these two phenomena is the existence of a professional culture which supports strong professional ties between teachers. These ties are sustained by frequent, informal and formal interaction, social ease and professional discourse. Such processes are characterised by and sustain professional openness, security and trust which nurture the willingness of individuals to face up to professional differences and the capacity to deal with these differences productively. These are some of the cultural 'nutrients' (Whitaker 1997) which support the growth of workplace conditions for staff to learn professionally with and from one another. They also displace the cultural toxins which can otherwise pollute personal relations in schools. Cultural toxins undermine the confidence of teachers to talk honestly by allowing negative micro-political undercurrents to develop.

While a collaborative culture is important for creating a psychological climate conducive to professional learning and growth, such a culture is produced, in part, by and through organisational structures and systems. The key to self-improving schools is the development, at the school level, of certain organisational conditions – structures and systems – which generate the internal capacity for staff to benefit professionally from working with one another. Moreover, there is considerable empirical evidence from the projects reviewed here to support this perspective. In other words, persistent self-renewal, which is becoming more and more crucial to a school's success, is strongly associated with developing the capacity for staff to learn with and from one another and for them to take responsibility for one another's professional learning as well as for their own.

Much of the foregoing research is also supported by the educational literature focusing on school culture, school improvement and learning schools. Work in North America, for example, suggests that school improvement is achieved when teachers engage in continuous and precise talk about teaching practice, observe one another's teaching and provide feedback to one another, plan, prepare, research and evaluate teaching materials together and teach one another the practice of teaching (Little 1981: 12–13). Therefore, while in this section I have concentrated on my own research, it is supported by a larger body of empirical and scholarly research.

Structures, systems, culture and learning schools

At present learning schools are viewed as organizations characterised by work-based, collaborative professional learning among teachers. The school as a workplace typically reflects and supports a professional culture of interdependence in which teamwork and the sharing of ideas, plans, professional puzzles and problems are common. There is also an emphasis on the collection and use of evidence about pupils' learning and teaching. Many informal and some more formal attempts have been made to research action through observation and systems of auditing, monitoring and evaluation. While some of the evidence collected will be used for purposes of accountability, the major reason for collecting information is to increase awareness, knowledge and understanding about what is actually happening in the school and classrooms. Furthermore, all this activity is founded on an educative, developmental intent that underscores the whole business of looking at and making sense of what teachers and pupils are achieving. The point of this work is to create a learning environment for all staff enabling them to continuously improve the quality of the children's learning and the teachers' pedagogy.

Professional conversations and dialogues, informed by a knowledge of what is actually taking place stimulate on-the-job learning. Staffroom talk, the sharing of ideas and plans, opportunities for peer observation and collegial feedback provide a variety of contexts for osmotic learning by individuals and groups of teachers. When these are complemented and supplemented by carefully designed and executed staff development activities in the school, as well as by opportunities for off-site learning, then relatively high-powered, school-based teacher development becomes the norm. Although in such schools there will be a mix of incidental and planned developments occurring simultaneously, when these processes are managed – usually by the head teacher but also other leaders – the school as a workplace then becomes a rich, powerful learning environment for the teachers as well as for the pupils.

If this summarises the main features of how we think primary schools learn, the picture does not provide us with much more than an anatomical sketch. There are likely to be other features we have yet to discover or explore in greater depth before we can say with confidence that we have a detailed portrait of learning schools.

There are many signs that staff in primary schools are focusing on pupils' learning – their achievements, outcomes and progress. Indeed, in England head teachers and teachers are examining and evaluating pupil learning information more than ever before. Yet we need to ask whether such self-evaluation makes for a learning school. Using an evidence-informed approach and being critical of one's practice may be *elements* of a learning school, but they are insufficient to make it a learning one. Neither is it likely that schools with well-developed staff development strategies warrant the title 'learning school'. What the discussion here shows is that a combination of structures and systems need to be present and active.

The empirical evidence from the primary school projects reviewed in this chapter points to increasing attention being paid to pupils' learning, sometimes including asking the children for their views about their learning. However, there appears to be much less of an emphasis on learning about teaching. In some schools there are signs of this happening, but in my experience the current position is that little collaborative work among teachers is directly concerned with improving pedagogy. Moreover, it seems to me that when staff engage in the creation of professional knowledge it cannot be assumed that this will necessarily enhance teachers' pedagogic performance.

If schools are to meet the many challenges they face and to become self-renewing organizations capable of managing both educational change and their improvement efforts, they will most likely need to become learning schools in which explicit craft knowledge is created, validated and disseminated about both pupils' learning and pedagogy. As such they will need to become not only learning schools but also *teaching schools*: that is, schools where, over time, teachers consciously and collaboratively develop deeper understandings and more highly accomplished pedagogic practices as well as similarly rich insights into the nature of pupils' learning. The two go together, particularly when teachers examine and enhance their teaching through the lens of pupils' learning.

In the literature there is advocacy for this dual focus between learning and teaching to be sustained, yet there is little hard evidence that it always happens. Empirical research in Birmingham and Essex LEAs suggests that it can take place, but not necessarily in all schools. This has prompted me to explore the pathways by which schools may become learning and teaching organizations (see Figure 6.1).

Given all of the foregoing it seems to me that creating learning and teaching schools takes time and starts with leaders establishing certain key structures and systems which, in turn, influence how staff interact. Also, to ensure professional collaboration and learning leaders should design and guide the process. In line with the argument in Chapter 5, they should lead by example, monitor the organizational processes and engage staff in dialogue. This is what Figure 6.1 tries to capture, suggesting a phased process of development.

The figure starts from a formalised approach to school self-evaluation and 'moves' through different phases of development. The second phase includes enhanced levels of co-operative practices between teachers, while the third marks a move to more fully-formed patterns of an interactive, collaborative culture.

Learning schools in the fourth phase are typified by an explicit goal to increase professional learning and by staff taking responsibility for the learning of other adults. Moreover, the creation of craft knowledge will be managed so that individuals and subgroups' professional development is disseminated to others inside and, when appropriate, beyond the school. Formal and informal *learning networks* will be a feature of such schools.

However, the learning and teaching school is not only the fifth phase but the one that embodies all the other four. As Figure 6.1 attempts to capture, each subsequent phase includes the attributes of the previous ones. In this way the process of development is incremental and nested, though nothing like as straightforward as suggested in Figure 6.1. The process is likely to involve much more dynamic movements than this model can show. It is also likely that such schools will have restructured and re-cultured themselves along the way.

Therefore, learning and teaching schools will appear similar to the learning school. Yet learning and teaching schools will be differentiated by the degree of

Formal self-evaluating school
- Monitoring and using evidence
- Action planning and targets
- Targeted actions
- Progress checks and evaluation

Teacher cooperation and interaction
- Joint planning
- Sharing
- Classroom visiting
- Benchmarking
- Subject leaders monitoring
- Contrived collegiality

Collaborative teacher culture
- Formal and informal dialogue
- Whole-school policies fully implemented
- High level of consistency
- Dialogue, debate, differences, challenge
- Teamwork
- Pupil perspectives sought

Learning school
- Staff sharing to learn, as well as know
- Mentoring, coaching
- School-based CPD
- Achievements of pupils, individual staff and staff groups identified
- External perspectives sought and accepted, external networking
- Feedback loops

Learning and teaching schools
- Analysis of teaching strengths and needs by all
- Development of pedagogy a norm
- Development of teaching informed by analysis of pupil learning
- Strengthening teaching a corporate responsibility
- Teachers teach teachers
- Teachers learning about learning

Figure 6.1 Developing learning and teaching schools

emphasis they place on pedagogy and the extent to which they act on this knowledge. Hence activities such as mentoring, supervision and coaching will be widespread and used by and for all staff, rather than just beginning teachers. They may also be characterised by clear signs that staff in these schools apply their new knowledge to their professional practice and act on it. Learning and teaching schools are likely to be places where there is a strong expectation – communicated directly and indirectly – that teachers will develop their skills over time and that they can play a part in improving colleagues' practice through peer coaching and in being coached themselves. They are likely to be schools in which teachers learn with and from one another and where they openly teach one another.

We have learned much about teacher cultures, staff development and school improvement over the last two decades, although there will always be more to know. In some respects we may now have reached a stage where we have a reasonably clear idea about some – perhaps many – of the building blocks of how schools learn. If so the puzzle we now face is how to fit them together. The figure offered here is but a stimulus to trying to solve that problem.

However, it is likely that because schools are social organizations, sometimes being non-rational environments and unpredictable places, they will not develop as learning and teaching schools in a linear, sequential fashion. Recent thinking in the business world suggests that the way the component parts fit together and build learning organizations is not in a mechanical or orderly fashion but in non-linear ways. According to Nonaka and Takeuchi's (1995) analysis of the knowledge-creating company, the linear model of knowledge creation is displaced by a number of *interactive* networks which reflect complex forms of negotiation and interaction between people, some of whom will offer different kinds of knowledge. Therefore, existing notions of organization may need to be revised because learning and teaching schools may be arranged more as knowledge and learning networks which are flexible, based on teams and whose boundaries are blurred and overlap with others inside and outside the school.

In closing this section there is one other point to make. The importance of organizational structures and systems rests on two issues. The first is that they are strongly implicated in leadership. School structures are leadership processes and pathways. Second, they simultaneously create ways of working which facilitate organizational resilience, reliability, learning and growth. That is, they make schools not only more efficient but also more effective. The heads who talked about structures and systems in the three school-size projects implicitly knew this. Thus they worked hard to put in place all the various policies and procedures because they knew that by doing so they were strengthening their own and their colleagues' leadership and learning as well as that of the pupils.

School-size effects

The ideas presented so far are generalized ones which assume that all primary schools are similar. Of course, this book does not take this stance and aims to provide a more differentiated picture of primary schools, leadership and improvement. With this goal in mind it is now necessary to examine what has gone before and identify how school size alters the picture offered here. A more textured interpretation of the general picture is needed.

It seems to me that in small schools, where personal contact is relatively high compared to large schools, leaders will be able to establish organizational structures and systems and given consent amongst the staff to implement these and adhere to them. They are likely to be enacted in a more informal way than in larger schools. The small size of the staff group facilitates less formal discourse than in larger groups. Yet there are dangers here. Informality may invoke a more casual approach which could undermine the purpose of staff talking to one another and compromise the implementation of agreed plans.

Leaders in small schools thus need to monitor the relationship between:

• Informal discourse
• The extent to which this talk is professional or not
• Whether dialogue is leading to pedagogic learning
• Whether teacher developments are transferred into classroom changes and improvements.

Indeed, these links should be monitored by all leaders in all schools regardless of their size. Leaders of learning and teaching schools need to attend not only to creating the school as learning environment for the adults as well as the children, but also to gauging what, if any, are the learning outcomes for their staff. However, the more informality is the norm in the workplace, the more this should be scrutinized to see if it supports school growth and better classroom practices.

Nor is this notion of informality in small schools meant to convey that formality should be entirely absent. The very idea of structure means that things are organized, planned and recorded, yet these need not be done in a bureaucratic way. The size of the staff group in small schools tends to mean that they can work together in ways characterized by social ease, friendliness and good humour. These qualities should help sustain the group dynamic and make them active, learning sets.

In medium-sized schools, particularly those with up to ten teachers, the staff group can largely work together and sustain a sense of 'whole school'. However, while informality will be present, it is likely that greater formality will be needed than in smaller schools. This is particularly true when new staff join the group. Informality can be so strong that sometimes newcomers feel excluded. Moreover, arrangements will need to be planned so that all know who is expected to do what and when.

As the size of medium schools increases then once the staff group exceeds, say, twelve teachers it becomes harder to sustain the whole staff-group dynamic. Thus for some discussions smaller groups need to be created and led. These might be Key Stage teams, though not always, since across-school groups also have their place, especially if 'Balkanization' (Hargreaves: 1994) is to be avoided. Balkanization refers to staff groups fragmenting into factions. A Balkanized culture is one where staff collaborate, but only within their subgroups. In Balkanized schools, staff groups do not collaborate and there is unhealthy competition and rivalry between them.

In larger medium-sized schools and in all large and very large schools, structural arrangements need to be evaluated on their effectiveness and on the way they shape and influence collaboration, trust and professional learning. Organizational structures may divide, create fragmentation and cause Balkanized relations, thereby ensuring that some staff are unable to learn from certain other colleagues because they never meet them, work with them, or because they have grown apart and distant from each other. Groupings separate staff, and one casualty may be trust and openness. Leaders thus need to monitor the social capital across and between groups as well as inside them. This is likely to apply in particular to the SMT and the rest of the staff. In some circumstances fault lines can open up between staff and the SMT.

In large and very large schools, therefore, mechanisms are needed to bring the groups together, to remix them so that, over time, everyone has a chance to work with everyone else and for individuals to lead a variety of groups. It will also be important for leaders to use small groupings. Insisting on staff working in threes and fours may be highly beneficial and much more preferable to staff working in a group of twenty-five or thirty teachers. This is particularly true when the purpose of the gathering is professional learning. If the meeting is a factual, briefing event, large gatherings are efficient. However, if the purpose of the discussion is to learn with and from others then smaller learning sets are much more advantageous. Thus in large schools networks of staff become necessary. School leaders need to orchestrate these and ensure that groups remain active and interactive learning arenas.

The effect of school size, therefore, is to increase leaders' awareness of the social dynamic of the groups they create. School structures and systems need to be fine-tuned to ensure they create and sustain trust, and thus contribute to the social capital of the staff. Unless they do, there may be much talk about professional learning but few signs of it actually taking place.

Conclusions

The discussion in this chapter has travelled some way from its starting point. I have tried to develop the argument that organisational structures and systems alter the nature and content of leadership. Structures and systems should be aimed at supporting leadership by providing a context for leaders to work with staff in ways that maximise the potential of colleagues and leaders alike. In so doing, seven points emerge which need to highlighted here.

Organisational arrangements, first of all, are important because they reduce the focus on 'the leader' and increase attention on creating the organisational conditions for leadership across the school.

Secondly, I argued that they ensure consistency of classroom practice among teachers. In effect I was saying that structures move schools away from reliance on the individual head teacher or leader by establishing ways of working that function whether the individual is present or not. In other words, structures and systems help schools become high reliability organisations. Regardless of who is there, systems ensure that common procedures are followed and the school proceeds on an even keel.

Thirdly, some systems were seen to be particularly important to the health and vitality of the school. These were arrangements for monitoring classrooms, planning processes, the use of pupil learning data, school self-evaluation, target-setting and policies for learning and for teaching, as well as communication structures and systems which brought colleagues together to talk, share and analyse their practices.

Fourthly, such systems rely on and simultaneously produce a particular form of teacher culture. Collaborative cultures characterized by high levels of security, openness and trust create a workplace environment for enriched, professional learning. Professional learning which is focused on improving pupils' learning and the quality of teaching is central to school improvement.

Fifthly, although this outlook is shared by many researchers and practitioners alike, too little attention has been paid to how schools transform themselves into such organizations. I therefore argued, on the basis of a series of related primary school improvement projects that there was a process of development, which started from school self-evaluation and worked towards their becoming learn-ing and teaching organisations. Learning and teaching schools are advanced, sophisticated workplaces. While every school should aspire to become such an organization, the process takes time and is probably phased. Figure 6.1 is but a simple outline of what the process involves and looks like. It may also prompt leaders to consider where their schools presently are in terms of their develop-ment journeys.

Sixthly, learning and teaching schools also place other demands on leaders. As Senge (1990) has said of learning organizations, leaders in such schools are not heroes or heroines. Such myths reinforce a focus on short-term events and charisma, rather than on systemic forces and collective learning:

> The new view of leadership in learning organizations centres on subtler and more important tasks. In a learning organization, leaders are designers, stewards and teachers. They are responsible for building organizations where people continually expand their capabilities . . . that is, they are responsible for learning.
>
> (p. 340)

Thus leaders need to design structures and systems that ensure important work gets done in ways that are simultaneously educative and developmental for everyone – pupils, staff and leaders. Thus leaders need to see themselves and the structures and systems they design as contributing to their role as learning

architects for the school. Leadership is thus about 'designing the learning processes whereby people throughout the organization can deal productively with
the critical issues they face' (p. 345).

Seventh, and following on from the last point, leaders therefore need to attend
to the social and interpersonal dynamics of the school and the staff groups of the
school. These groupings are influenced by the size of the school and as the
number of subgroups increases, so too do leaders need to consider the dangers of
fragmentation and its effects on staff learning. This involves not only seeing the
different structures and systems as pieces but also as a whole. It is not just about
rearranging the organizational structures, 'it is also about understanding wholes'
(p. 343).

These seven points together mean that the work of school leaders is changing.
These changes mean that school leaders have new and emerging development
needs and that these vary according to the size of the school they work in. The
next chapter therefore looks at leadership development.

7 Developing leaders and leadership

The focus of this chapter could easily form another book. Leadership development is a large topic covering many areas, and there is a considerable body of research, both national and international to draw upon to fully understand the issues, as we learned during our work at the National College for School Leadership. Given the range and depth of knowledge I could draw upon, I am going to try to keep the discussion relatively brief and focused on the issues already addressed or touched upon in the previous chapters. Therefore this chapter is far from being a comprehensive treatment of the field.

The chapter is organised into three main sections. In the first I discuss what the research into small, medium-sized and large primary schools implies for developing leaders of these different school sizes. To do this, I shall focus on three groups of leaders: heads, deputies and subject leaders or coordinators. The second section looks at learning-centred leadership. Here I elaborate a little more on the idea introduced in Chapter 5 before discussing what it implies for leadership development in schools. The third section looks at developing leadership in schools, and the focus here is essentially upon building leadership capacity within schools.

Developing leaders

In the previous chapters I reported that heads and deputies generally believed they had learned most about leading schools by doing it. This viewpoint has a long tradition, though whether it will continue is open to question. Very few of the heads included in the three studies reported in this book had undertaken the National Professional Qualification for Headship (NPQH) programme and only a handful had completed the Leadership Programme for Serving Heads (LPSH). When research has examined the impact of these programmes and others the NCSL is piloting, alongside those courses higher education and LEAs provide, we might begin to see how the power of on-the-job learning is augmented by them. Then many more leaders than at present should be better placed to explain whether and how on-the-job learning is enhanced by out-of-school learning activities.

Given this general viewpoint, I shall now examine in turn what are the main lessons about leadership development for heads, deputies and subject leaders in primary schools of different sizes.

Head-teacher development

The idea that learning about leadership is achieved only by doing it is one which deserves to be challenged rather than simply be taken at face value. I do not doubt that it is the most common form of leadership learning, but that does not mean it is the most effective or the best. Experience can be a powerful teacher, but it does not automatically follow that we all learn, or always learn, from experience. Moreover, as has been reported earlier, experiential learning can be negative as well as positive.

I do not want to argue that experiential learning is ineffective. However, I do wish to suggest that it can be made more powerful when it occurs in combination with other forms of learning. The experience of leading a team, or school, provides individuals with much to reflect on. Reflecting on these experiences is a vital part of learning from them. Moreover, analysing and thinking through what happened and why, with a colleague, or in a group, frequently deepens the learning process. One reason why this is true is because when we discuss an event or incident with others we start to co-construct new insights, understandings and knowledge. Reflection as a social activity provides the conditions for the co-creation of craft knowledge. It also encourages and supports transformative learning, as discussed briefly in Chapter 5.

Therefore this line of reasoning points to heads and other leaders benefiting from mentoring partnerships, coaching and participating in local support groups as well as online learning communities. Such arrangements provide opportunities to articulate what has been happening and to delve beneath the surface of incidents and issues that individuals may be trying to come to terms with, comprehend and resolve.

In terms of school size, it seems to me that it is very important that heads in small schools are enabled to do this. In small schools the relative lack of other leaders makes their heads quite isolated. While many such heads enjoy excellent professional relations with staff, this does not necessarily translate into their being able to discuss their leadership problems and puzzles with their workplace colleagues. In the smallest of schools, which have no deputy, there is often no one to bounce ideas off, to share concerns with or talk through options and decisions with. It is no surprise to me that heads of many small schools develop partnerships with local heads, form support groups, rely on LEA staff or find their own mentors. All these tactics are antidotes to the loneliness leaders experience.

While these arrangements are important in all kinds of ways, this is not to say they are always – or ever – learning forums. There is an important place within these groupings for heads to use them to learn with and from one another, not in an incidental or accidental way but in a planned and formal manner.

Heads of medium-sized and large schools are likely to have leadership colleagues they can learn alongside. Here I am thinking of deputy heads. Productive partnerships of heads and deputies often involve their becoming learning pairs, as research in the 1990s suggests (Southworth 1998). However, there are examples of heads and deputies not working like this. Some simply do not 'get on'; while others fail to use their working arrangements to enhance their learning. Also, some heads tend to treat the learning as a one-way process. Heads may see themselves as mentors and coaches to their deputy partners but do not expect or acknowledge that this flow could be reversed and the learning reciprocated. If more heads and deputies approached their work as mutual learning, as well as task completion, there would probably be more experiential leadership learning taking place in schools.

In the larger schools, management and leadership teams offer increased opportunities for leadership learning and for this to be a shared and social process. However, as alluded to in the previous paragraph, we need to see learning as not necessarily attached to positions and the hierarchy of the school. Heads do not always know more than other colleagues, and they should avoid presenting themselves as such. Indeed, one of the most enabling ways of enriching professional learning in schools is when heads explicitly acknowledge that they are learners and model this for their colleagues (Nias *et al.* 1992).

Thus we can trace the outlines of in-school and out-of-school leadership learning and see how in schools of different sizes different emphases may be valid. This, though, overlooks the fact that many heads also see their leadership development as staged in terms of the number of headships they take on.

A significant proportion of heads start off in small schools and work their way to larger ones. Some therefore take on two or three headships in different-sized schools, which may also vary by their socio-economic settings and performance levels. I have suggested that as heads travel from one school to another they need to pay attention to the different leadership emphases which schools of different size create.

In small schools, heads can exercise more direct leadership and expect to influence more strongly the teaching and learning in colleagues' classrooms, because there are fewer of them than in larger schools, and the head's example is less distant and diluted. In small schools, the head is most clearly the head *teacher* – in fact, they are often the lead teacher.

In medium-sized schools heads should develop shared leadership with their deputies and senior teachers. This means their individual and direct influence is somewhat lower than in smaller schools and needs to be counterbalanced by deploying more leaders. In other words, as the head's personal, direct influence 'decreases', other leaders' direct and indirect leadership needs to increase.

Such a balance is even more prevalent in large primary schools. Here heads have to work through others: deputies, members of the SMT and year-group leaders. Therefore, heads must take responsibility for developing other leaders. In effect, heads in larger primary schools are leaders of leaders. They must create the conditions for lots to lead and for leadership at all levels. In large and very large schools, a head's personal influence will be relatively small in terms of them influencing what goes on in classrooms. Yet, in turn, they must ensure that others are able to take on this role, and heads and maybe other senior leaders must support and develop these 'middle leaders' to influence the quality of teaching and learning.

This hurried sketch of the way size alters the nature of headship in schools of different sizes creates a continuum from heads being direct and indirect learning-centred leaders in small schools to heads being indirect leaders who develop learning-centred leadership amongst colleagues in large schools. The change is from heads as individuals exercising learning-centred leadership to developing other leaders to do it.

However, in setting out this continuum it may be too simple to assume that every head can make the change from individually doing learning-centred leadership to enabling others to do it. The difference between doing it and facilitating others to do it is a big one. As educators, heads are well placed to be able to teach others to lead, since they are capable teachers and accustomed to working with other adults. However, we should not presume that this role appeals to every head, nor that every head can do it. All that has been set out here is the idea that such a shift takes place and that those who move from one school to a larger one need to be aware of these differences in role and responsibilities.

Deputy head-teacher development

Deputies are reliant on their head teacher partners to act as leadership models and coaches to them. We have known this for a long time, but it does not seem to have radically altered the fact that many deputies are neither enabled to lead by their headteacher colleagues nor always provided with positive role models. Consequently, deputy headship is often an underpowered role in primary schools. We urgently need to remedy this state of affairs.

Some encouraging signs are emerging which suggest that primary school deputies are taking on more responsibilities, but there is probably still some way to go before we can be confident that this role in primary schools is a fulfilling and strategically important one. When working with groups of deputies I meet many who describe how they work in partnership with their head-teacher colleagues, and some of these pairings are plainly professionally productive and dynamic. Yet I also encounter some who are not permitted to take a lead. Their role is essentially that of day-to-day management, and they rarely exercise leadership – even when the head is absent. These deputies characterise their role when acting head as that of a 'caretaker' who keeps the school running smoothly until the head returns. These individuals are allowed only to manage, not to take a lead. Such a situation is neither good preparation for headship nor does it empower the deputy so that the school benefits from the best that individual can offer.

I do not doubt that deputies and other leaders need to know how to manage schools. There is much to manage in schools today, and too much leadership and too little management is as inappropriate as too much management and too little leadership. If deputies need to be knowledgeable about management, it also follows from what has been argued in previous chapters that they also need to develop their abilities to exercise learning-centred leadership.

In smaller and medium-sized schools a positive and productive partnership with the head is critical to the health and vitality of the school and to the relationships of staff members with one another. Shared leadership should provide the basis for both the deputy and the head to strengthen their on-the-job professional learning. Heads should certainly mentor their deputies, at the same time acknowledging that such support will also develop themselves in their role. There is also scope for heads to coach their deputy-head partners from time to time. The National College for School Leadership is committed to strengthening leadership coaching in schools, and heads and deputies are an obvious starting point for this work. In the best partnerships it already takes place; the next stage is to increase the level of its adoption.

When heads mentor and coach their deputy-head partners, the message that is conveyed to all staff is that here are colleagues who believe in professional development, who see their roles as learning opportunities and who strive to learn with and from one another. Such messages are vital if we are to create and sustain our schools as learning organisations.

While this creates a wealth of learning opportunities in schools for deputies, these also need to be supplemented by off-site development activities. Here I have in mind deputy-head support groups, LEA and HE courses and the NPQH programme. All of these, over time, should supplement and complement the professional development of deputies.

In the larger schools, though, all this development work needs to embrace another aspect of the role. Deputies in large schools should, alongside their heads, act as coaches to middle leaders. For those new to the post this may not be appropriate in the first year of deputy headship, but once established they will need to work alongside their heads to ensure both are building the leadership capacity in their school. The more leadership is distributed, the more leaders need to be developed.

Developing other leaders is hardly something which is acknowledged in the literature on primary deputy headship. Indeed, it has only come to light as a result of the study reported here and my examination of the implications of the findings, though neither would have been brought to prominence without the increase in the number of large schools and their becoming worthy of attention.

Therefore in terms of the differences between smaller and larger schools, the significant one that occurs in the case of deputies is a mirror image of that involving heads. The larger the school, the more the deputy needs to take responsibility for the professional development of other leaders. However, it is also likely to be the case that deputies will exercise learning-centred leadership more than their head teacher colleagues, so that deputies' direct leadership effects may be more prolonged than those of heads.

Subject leadership development

Subject leaders, managers or curriculum coordinators (we have never agreed a single title for this role) have been shown to play important roles in all sizes of schools, although in the largest ones they are not as prominent as leaders of organisational units and sub-units. Nevertheless, for this subsection I shall include all other school leaders.

What emerges from the discussion so far and from previous chapters is that these individuals need to play a greater and more effective leadership role than formerly. This I typify as learning-centred leadership, but rather than explore what this is – which the next section will do – here I simply wish to reinforce the point that it is the need of these subject coordinators to take a lead which should now be given a higher profile.

If we are serious about distributed leadership and ensuring there is sufficient leadership density to influence and improve the quality of teaching and learning in every classroom across the school, then outside the smallest schools this means increasing the power of 'middle leaders'. Such an outlook means, in turn, that they need to be mentored, coached and developed, and this is why I have laboured the point about changing the roles of heads and deputies to meet this need. Moreover, there may also be a need to alter the teacher cultures in some schools because there still lingers the belief that only the head can instruct teachers what to do. Such an outlook undermines and inhibits deputy heads and coordinators who feel in such contexts that they cannot directly advise, monitor feedback or intervene with teacher colleagues. In short, such an outlook undermines teacher leadership.

Therefore, if we want to develop distributed leadership we should seek to support individual middle leaders, provide them with opportunities to lead, and ensure colleagues know and understand that these leaders have the full backing of the head and governors. Heads must ensure they create permitting circumstances for others to lead.

Learning-centred leadership

In Chapter 5 I argued that school leadership is essentially about teaching and learning or – as North Americans say – instructional leadership. My stance reflects professional experience of headship, research I have conducted into primary headship and the views of numerous scholars in this country and internationally. For example, Richard Elmore, in an important paper in the United States, has argued that we should 'focus leadership on instructional improvement and define everything else as instrumental to it' (Elmore 2000: 14). Under this definition, the skills and knowledge that matter in leadership 'are those that can be connected to, or lead directly to, the improvement of instruction and student performance ... It makes leadership instrumental to improvement' (p. 14).

I have already said that many heads do not like the notion of 'instructional leadership', and neither do I. The term implies too strong a focus on teaching and appears to ignore learning. By contrast the concept of 'learning-centred leadership' concentrates on the improvement of learning and teaching. It seeks to enhance the quality of learning through analysing pupils' learning processes and outcomes and by drawing upon contemporary ideas and knowledge about learning (e.g. formative assessment, constructivist concepts of learning), intelligence, and developing pedagogy in the light of all this information.

Learning lies at the heart of school leadership, improvement and transformation. Much of the twentieth century was preoccupied with teaching. Educational debates revolved around (and around!) what to teach. A great deal of time and effort were devoted to the curriculum as content, to questions of what pupils needed to know and to how we should assess whether they had acquired this knowledge. Unsurprisingly a transmission model of teaching and learning underscored much of what went on and still goes on.

Lately we have recognised that more attention should be paid to pupils' learning. Contemporary thinking shows that learning is not merely the absorption of knowledge but an active process of the mind. Learning is about constructing meaning and understanding; it is about students making sense – intellectually and emotionally – of the world. The emphasis is less on 'putting information in' and more on expanding existing knowledge, with the goal of children constructing new understandings.

Furthermore, the social context in which learning takes place is important. Talking with others is particularly powerful. As I argued in Chapter 5, dialogue stimulates analysis, reflection and the reorganisation of knowledge, enabling the learner to review their learning and relate it to previous experiences and understandings. Conversation and group discussion have a vital part to play in the learning process.

Another way of describing these ideas is to say that not only should we pay attention to how pupils learn but to helping them learn how to learn. However, two points need to highlighted. First, I am arguing for a shift in *emphasis*, not advocating that teaching is ignored. Indeed, quite the reverse is true because we should review our teaching through the lens of learners' experiences and outcomes. Second, changing the balance between teaching as transmission and teaching which enables pupils to construct new knowledge and become powerful learners is a process which needs to be led.

The concept of learning-centred leadership regards leadership as a social influencing process where leaders work with and through others. School leaders' direct effects on classrooms are small and decrease as the school increases in size. By contrast, their indirect effects are high because leadership is, in large measure, mediated through others. I argued in Chapter 5 that to exercise high levels of influence leaders need to work directly on their indirect effects, and by using three tactics which, in combination, are effective forms of influence upon teachers:

Modelling   – the power of example
Monitoring – paying attention to what is happening in classrooms and analysing classroom processes
Dialogue   – talking to teachers about learning and teaching, providing feedback to teachers on their practice and performance.

These three forms of influence are important because they enable professional learning. Observation and discussion are two of the most important ways we learn. Watching an able leader at work and noting how they deal with any problems they encounter can provide important windows into effective leadership in action. Discussing one's professional practice with a colleague facilitates analysis, articulation and the creation of new or richer craft knowledge.

What I am outlining here is an approach to leadership in which the medium of leadership – professional learning – is also the message. That is why it is called learning-centred: it is concerned not only with pupils' growth but also with learning on the part of the staff and leaders. Modelling, monitoring and dialogue shape what happens in classrooms and thinking in staffrooms. They help leaders at all levels to concentrate on pupil learning and use this as a basis for professional development. This is particularly true when colleagues examine their pedagogy through the lens of the children's learning. Then we move from thinking about learning and teaching, to thinking about *teaching for learning*.

The evidence and my own thinking in Chapters 5 and 6 suggest that changes in classrooms rest upon leaders focusing on six, interrelated levels of learning:

1   Pupil learning
2   Teacher learning
3   Collaborative staff learning
4   Organisational learning
5   Leadership learning
6   Learning networks

Pupil learning

The first level I have already reviewed. However, what is important to stress here is that in the great majority of cases such leadership involves using outcome data and monitoring what is happening in classrooms in a spirit of peer development. It also requires professional dialogues in which excellence is recognised, assumptions are challenged and new professional knowledge is created. It is a constructive and developmental process rather than a merely judgemental one. It is also an audit of professional skills and the knowledge needs of colleagues. It should reveal who is good at what aspects of teaching and who has a deep understanding of pupils' learning. Such information then becomes a basis for sharing this knowledge across the whole staff group. The process is thus diagnostic because it provides insights into who might lead the professional development of colleagues' pedagogy.

Teacher learning

Professional dialogues based on observation of classroom practices are significant forms of learning. Yet whilst necessary, such learning is not sufficient. Professional learning is vital, but it is just one piece in the process of changing practice. Certainly, enhanced craft knowledge and a deeper understanding of classroom dynamics are important outcomes, but only if they lead to improvements for pupils. The main purpose of professional dialogue is to enable participants to make their teaching and the pupils' learning more powerful. This is not to discount other benefits, such as peer support, collaborative teacher cultures and wider frames of reference. However, it is often the case that these latter benefits fail to reach the goal of doing the job better. We need to ensure that all who use this approach understand that the process seeks to improve classroom practices.

Learning-centred leadership is not being advocated here because it improves professional capacity; I am arguing that it needs to be used to heighten pupils' skills and capacities. As others have argued, unless we address the impact of such an approach on the pupils' progress we may only focus more attention on effects at the teacher level than at the level of the pupil (Huberman 1992: 11). There need to be learning outcomes for the teachers which are then applied in classrooms to enhance pupils' learning.

Therefore, throughout the observation, discussions and developmental meetings which flow around and through learning-centred leadership, it needs to be made plain that the new insights and ideas staff create or acquire should lead to changed practices in classrooms. In turn, leaders need to monitor whether and how colleagues are putting their new knowledge into practice.

Collaborative staff learning

The third level of learning is that of groups of teachers developing collaboratively. There is a considerable body of research evidence to support this position (e.g. Rosenholtz 1989; Nias *et al.* 1992; Fullan and Hargreaves 1992). Teacher development groups might, in small schools, be the whole school staff, the teaching staff in medium-sized schools, as well as structural units such as Key Stage teams, departments of teachers, or year groups in medium-sized and large schools. In some schools teachers get together in alternative groupings and form their own learning teams or action learning sets. These informal teams can be valuable in that they supplement established structural arrangements and transcend subject or other boundaries in the school. Whatever the groupings and the arrangements for them, ensuring that professional learning takes place collaboratively is essential. Moreover, these groupings provide arenas for teachers who have been identified by the leaders as possessing specific skills and success in their teaching to share them with their colleagues. Teachers thus teach their teacher colleagues and the group becomes a team which is greater than the sum of its parts.

Organisational learning

Fourth, the school becomes a learning organisation. The literature on learning schools is large and shows them to be relatively advanced forms of social organisation (e.g. Senge 1990; Fullan 1993; Leithwood and Seashore Louis 1998; Southworth 2000). Such schools are characterised by climates of trust, openness and security (Nias *et al.* 1992). Trust is essential if people are to work together, learn from one another and apply their learning in classrooms. Without trust colleagues lack the confidence to talk openly with one another because they are fearful of negative or even hostile reactions. An absence of trust undermines openness. Therefore, leaders need to think about creating in their schools the conditions that enable the workplace to be a positive, professional learning environment for the adults as well as the students.

Leadership learning

Creating learning schools rests, in large measure, on the quality of leadership. The more professional development and improvement takes place within a school, the more leaders are required to exercise learning-centred leadership. Thus leadership needs to be distributed to ensure there is sufficient of it to influence teaching and learning. Heads, deputies and assistant heads may well need to become leadership mentors and coaches to their colleagues. At the National College for School Leadership we are clear that distributed leadership means developing leadership which influences the quality of learning and teaching right across the school and at all levels.

Learning networks

The sixth level is the need for learning networks of schools. Without this level professional learning could be too strongly 'inside focused'. Without external input we may never rethink existing practices which we take for granted. Being able to engage with others outside the school helps us to see anew. We all need to look outside the confines of our contexts in order to see more clearly the strengths and limitations within them.

These six levels might appear to be in a sequential order; they are not. For example, individuals and groups can be involved in networks without the school becoming a learning organisation. Likewise leadership learning is needed to support each and every level. However, the backbone of this approach is that leaders visit classrooms, observe and discuss with teacher colleagues what they see and what the teacher is concerned about in their practice. Without this basic, hands-on, person-centred approach everything else is blighted. Thus interpersonal skills lie at the core of this work. Notwithstanding this key feature, the intention must be that over time all six levels of learning are achieved and operate simultaneously. Then we will have learning teachers, leaders, schools and systems.

There is one other issue to note. Learning-centred leadership rests not only on leaders being able to relate positively to colleagues, engage them in professional dialogues, listen actively to them and provide them with constructive feedback. It also needs leaders to be knowledgeable about learning and teaching. At the very least this means that heads, deputies and subject leaders must know about the learning and teaching requirements of the literacy and numeracy strategies, the OFSTED teaching observation schedules and criteria, and their schools' policies for learning, teaching and assessment. Beyond these areas leaders must also know about current thinking on learning and teaching, which is why the National College produced a series of 'learning texts' aimed at providing this knowledge for them.

Peter Hill, in a paper prepared for one of the National College's 'think tank' meetings on school leadership, argued that:

> Teaching and learning will change radically as educators fully internalise what it means to accept socially constructivist views of learning, to operate as members of a learning organisation and to take up the challenge of teaching for in-depth learning and the acquisition of high-level, generic skills of thinking, communicating and problem-solving. Similarly, after a slow start, the rapid take-up of new information and communication technologies in classrooms is leading to approaches to accessing and processing information that change forever the traditional role of the teacher as the source of information and knowledge . . .
>
> The head teacher and other key members of the leadership team will need to disseminate this new knowledge and become centrally involved in implementing processes to promote the ongoing professional learning of all staff members.
>
> (Hill 2001: 5)

These are important ideas, not least because they challenge any separation of headship from learning and teaching. Yet, we know that, over time, school leaders, particularly heads of medium-sized and large schools can become detached from classroom concerns. The last fifteen years have been times of great change when more and more has been expected of heads as leaders of complex organisations, but as leaders who may be less – rather than more – connected to the core business of the school, namely teaching and learning (Hill 2000: 3). When heads become distanced, let alone divorced from teaching and learning, this can undermine their professional leadership.

I would argue that all heads should remain in contact with classrooms, regardless of the size of the school. This outlook is strongly supported by school inspection evidence as well as by the research reported in Chapters 2 and 3. However, the nature of the contact may take several forms. It is obvious from earlier chapters that heads in small schools need to exercise a hands-on approach with all their teacher colleagues and on a regular, frequent basis. As the size of the school increases and deputy heads are in post, they too must be involved. Likewise subject leaders in medium-sized and large schools should exercise influence, and as they increase in number so does the amount of time heads and deputies devote to developing learning-centred leadership. In the largest schools, heads and deputies will be investing much of their leadership in leadership development. However, they should also demonstrate to colleagues that they are able to practise what they preach. Moreover, by exercising such leadership themselves they will keep in touch with teaching and learning inside classrooms. Learning-centred leadership offers an effective strategy for keeping heads in touch with and knowledgeable about classroom processes. And they can do this by observing and talking with colleagues; thus monitoring is simultaneously professional development for the observed colleague and the head teacher. It is imperative that we do not have educationally uninformed head teachers, and that translates into heads avoiding being detached from the learning and teaching.

Therefore, what heads and other senior leaders need to consider is both the extent to which they exercise such leadership and the balance they strike between doing it and developing other leaders to work in this way. Furthermore – and tying this discussion to the previous section – the development of such leadership will involve mentoring and coaching colleagues to do it. However, it should not be overlooked that in schools where the head is already a learning-centred leader, this provides a model for other emerging leaders to follow and thus the more learning-centred leadership is practised in a school, the easier it is to develop others.

Developing leadership capacity in schools

I will concentrate on three sets of points in this section: schools as learning organisations, distributed leadership and teacher culture. These three are interrelated and thus the sequence in which I discuss them is somewhat arbitrary.

At a number of points in this chapter and elsewhere I have argued that schools should be learning organisations. This means that attention needs to be paid to the school as a learning environment for the adults who work there. It also means that the school as a workplace should become a professional development workshop.

Schools as learning organisations

This viewpoint is consistent with the idea that leaders learn most about leadership by doing it. Although earlier I challenged the idea that on-the-job learning was necessarily the most effective form of professional learning, my position is that, given certain organisational conditions and out-of-school support, experiential learning is the most valuable form.

The organisational conditions which need to be present are as follows. There should be planned learning opportunities as well as serendipitous ones. Although much professional learning takes place informally and spontaneously, it should be accompanied by a more systematic, formalised approach as well. Learning-centred leadership in action may look opportunistic, and often it can be; but it should also be planned and structured. I know several heads who have developed simple rota systems to ensure they visit each teacher colleague in turn and spend similar amounts of time with them all. Moreover, collaborative learning sessions should be organised to ensure individual colleagues' strengths are shared across the staff group. Such planning should include opportunities for less experienced or emerging leaders to be coached and mentored by established leaders. There may also be occasions when outside consultants are involved. Advanced skills teachers, colleagues from other schools, LEA staff, literacy and numeracy support staff and advisers, as well as freelance consultants might be called upon to improve pedagogy or to train subject leaders.

The last sentence includes a particular emphasis which should not go unnoticed. I have slipped from a broad discussion about schools becoming learning organisations to one where I am thinking of them as leadership-learning environments. Although the two can largely go together, this shift in my focus is not accidental. If we wish to encourage leadership at all levels, then we need to create the conditions in school for leadership learning.

However, the first and foremost condition is opportunity. Leaders can be trained and prepared for their roles. They can be made knowledgeable and to gain great insight into the theories of leading and managing. Yet without the opportunity to lead all this prior learning counts for little. Heads and deputies must be willing, at some point, to encourage other colleagues to lead. Unless opportunities are created for colleagues to lead, shared leadership can never flourish.

This brings me to the second point. What I am talking about in terms of developing leadership capacity in primary schools is moving towards more distributed forms of leadership. Such leadership aims to improve the school through developing the quality of teaching and learning and:

> . . . differs from that typically described in the literature on management – leaders, or higher level managers, who exercise 'control' over certain functions in the organisation. There are, to be sure, certain routine organisational functions that require control – bus schedules, payroll, accounting, etc. But the term 'control' applied to school improvement is a dubious concept because one does not 'control' improvement processes as much as one guides them and provides direction for them, since most of the knowledge required for improvement must inevitably reside in the people who deliver instruction, not in the people who manage them. Control implies that the controller knows exactly what the controllee (if you will) should do, whereas guidance and direction imply some degree of shared expertise and some degree of difference in the level and kind of expertise among individuals. It is this problem of the distribution of knowledge required for

large scale improvement that creates the imperative for the development of models of distributed leadership.

(Elmore 2000: 14)

There is just too much to know about teaching and learning for any individual leader or teacher to hold a monopoly on craft knowledge. For this reason I advocate learning-centred leadership, because heads and other leaders need to know who knows what, who could benefit from each individual's teaching strengths and prowess and who should play a lead in managing and transferring professional knowledge across the school. As Elmore goes on to say:

> In a knowledge-intensive enterprise like teaching and learning, there is no way to perform these complex tasks without widely distributing the responsibility for leadership (again, guidance and direction) among roles in the organisation, and without working hard at creating a common culture, or set of values, symbols and rituals. Distributed leadership, then, means multiple sources of guidance and direction, following the contours of expertise in an organisation, made coherent through a common culture. It is the 'glue' of a common task or goal – improvement of instruction – and a common frame of values for how to approach that task – culture – that keeps distributed leadership from becoming another version of loose coupling.
>
> (Elmore 2000: 15)

The last point about loose coupling refers to the idea that schools have been for a long time fragmented organisations. Where teachers work in isolation from one another, never observe or visit another classroom or teacher and do not talk professionally about their practice, then the school is but a loose collection of relatively independent classrooms. English schools have moved a long way from this scenario, and learning-centred leadership should ensure we never return to it. That is one reason why I discussed the idea of leadership density in Chapter 5, speculated about the 'density index' and suggested that a leader-follower ratio of 1:4 was worth thinking about.

Distributed leadership

I agree with Elmore that 'the basic idea of distributed leadership is not very complicated' (p. 14). As he says:

> In any organised system, people typically specialise, or develop particular competencies, that are related to their predispositions, interests, aptitudes, prior knowledge, skills and specialised roles. Furthermore, in any organised system, competency varies considerably among people in similar roles; some principals and teachers, for example, are better at doing some things than others, either as a function of their personal preferences, their experience, or their knowledge. Organising these diverse competencies into a coherent

whole requires understanding how individuals vary, how the particular know-ledge and skill of one person can be made to complement that of another and how the competencies of some can be shared with others. In addition, organising diverse competencies requires understanding when the knowledge and skills possessed by the people within the organisation is not equal to the problem they are trying to solve, searching outside the organisation for new knowledge and skill and bringing it into the organisation.

(Elmore 2000: 14–15)

As noted a number of times above, distributed leadership is concerned with managing professional knowledge and skill in the school. What is distributed is not simply 'leadership' but a particular form, namely learning-centred leader-ship, because this embraces knowledge creation, management and transfer whilst, at the same time, improving the quality of teaching and learning.

Distributed leadership can also transcend formal, positional leadership. So far I have tended to associate the distribution of leadership to colleagues holding posts of responsibility – deputies, assistant heads and subject leaders. However, as these leaders identify colleagues with specific strengths which deserve to be shared with colleagues to enhance their practice, the individuals who are identified become teacher leaders. Once teachers are invited to share their strengths and lead discussions, workshops, seminars and, in effect, to lead by example, leader-ship becomes distributed in a way which breaks away from positional leadership.

Distributed leadership challenges the belief in 'the power of one' (Gronn 2000) – that is, the belief in the heroic, individual leader. It aims to move away from the power of one towards empowering everyone. Distributed leadership tied to organisational positions only moves leadership from one to a few more, whilst shared leadership may restrict it to just the head and deputy or to a handful of leaders in the senior management team. There may, of course, be good reasons for wanting to limit leadership to these few colleagues. However, let us not fool ourselves into thinking that this is fully fledged distributed leadership. That requires a relatively high incidence of positional leaders nurturing teacher leadership which moves around the group.

Teacher leadership will not only be a distributed form; it will also be more fluid and emergent than positional leadership. It will certainly not be fixed, as positional leadership might be (Gronn 2000: 11). And this begs questions about whether all or many heads will be comfortable with such flexibility. Those who prefer to control things may be discomfited by distributed leadership, but if it concentrates on improving the quality of learning and teaching, the trade-off for this discomfort should be a better performing school.

Teacher culture

This notion of distributed leadership almost certainly relies on a particular kind of teacher culture. Colleagues must be prepared to collaborate and be willing to learn with and from one another. The former is increasingly common, though the latter less certain, and leaders should be sure they do not confuse the two. Heads should be aware that the teacher culture they are creating and sustaining includes a relatively new element. Primary school cultures which support professional learning were examined in detail some time ago (e.g. Nias *et al.* 1992). However, the cultures we dissected then did not include much in the way of leadership learning. What I am suggesting now is that schools need to take greater responsibility for leadership development and thus grow their own leaders.

This is a relatively new emphasis and one which deserves detailed attention. It certainly involves heads and deputies letting go, and that can be a problem when the belief in the leader as a heroic figurehead holds sway in the school, the community or the mind of the head. Yet it also requires teachers to take hold of leadership opportunities when they are offered. Thus teachers who hold subject or coordinator responsibilities must be ready to act as leaders as well as managers. This means moving away from delegated management and towards distributed leadership, which is tied to positional duties. Such a shift cannot be assumed to happen smoothly in all cases.

Also, even when teachers are willing to lead, senior leaders may have to learn not only to let go but to follow. Asking someone to take a lead and letting them get on with it is all well and good, but it is likely to be but a part of the interpersonal dynamic. Inviting colleagues to lead workshops, meetings and training events will also require other senior leaders to attend and to follow their less experienced colleagues' direction and guidance. Again, some will find this difficult; yet it is important to do and to be seen doing. Heads and more experienced leaders should model their willingness to be influenced by others. Just as leading by example is important, so too is setting an example as a follower. The social dynamics of leadership and followership are subtle, sensitive and symbolic.

Despite these challenges, distributed leadership should enable all staff to take a lead from time to time and this, in turn, should enable leaders to emerge. Those who thrive on these opportunities may sooner, rather than later, seek out more opportunities or more formal roles. Even in medium-sized schools this should ensure that there are teachers ready to move into formal leadership positions when these become vacant. In the large and very large primary schools we studied, we heard that such succession planning and preparation was vital. Therefore, what appears to be not uncommon practice in large schools may need to spread to smaller ones.

Conclusions

I have discussed a number of key points in this chapter, and here I shall simply highlight the major ones.

The importance of on-the-job learning

What I have argued for is that this becomes more explicit than implicit. At present the learning which occurs whilst doing the job is not always sufficiently used as learning material. It is taken for granted. The general assumption is that we all learn from experience and therefore have little need for other learning opportunities or forms. My position is that we all learn from experience, but that we learn much more when we reflect on the experience and our actions and examine the consequences of what we decided and did. Mentors, coaches and learning partnerships can increase the power of experiential learning. Paradoxically, so too can off-the-job learning. Time out (as opposed to 'time off') from the bustle of work can be used to share experiences with peers, identify common issues and challenge assumptions and work habits. The work experiences we all collect need to become the content of our professional learning curricula, and our leadership colleagues in school need to become our tutors and consultants.

As the size of the school increases, so too does the responsibility on the headteacher to develop lots of other leaders

Building and sustaining the leadership capacity in the school is an emerging priority and one which primary heads should take more seriously than has often been the case in the past. The school size research reported in this book suggests that heads in primary schools can do this and that it needs to happen in relatively smaller-sized schools than has sometimes been assumed. The idea that the primary head is the sole leader in the school not only sustains the myth of the power of one; it also creates lonely leaders. Primary headship is changing from a pattern where one person dominates the school to a situation where many more leaders are playing their part alongside the head teacher. This trend needs to continue. Leadership at all levels – and especially increasing the power of middle leaders – is something heads and deputies should encourage, creating the conditions for this to happen.

Deputy heads need to be developed as leaders as well as managers

Heads must take the responsibility for coaching their deputy head colleagues, not least because no one else can or should do so. It is also the case that in some medium-sized schools and in all large and very large schools, deputy heads should coach the middle leaders. At present developing other leaders in the school is rarely seen as part of the deputy's role, nor is it something which has been acknowledged in the literature on deputy headship in primary schools. This is an idea whose time may have come, and it is something I would urge head and deputy colleagues in schools to take on.

Subject leaders should exercise rather more leadership than they do

Leading from the middle is important for all sorts of reasons, including: empowering those who have classroom expertise to spread theirs and colleagues' good practice across the school; increasing the leadership capacity in the school; valuing and recognising the skills and talents of teachers; moving leadership closer to the classroom level rather than pulling it away from teaching and learning. Increasing the influence of subject leaders lies at the heart of developing distributed leadership.

Learning-centred leadership is what matters most in schools

It is precisely this kind of leadership which should lie at the heart of school leadership, and everything else should be geared to facilitating it. Heads and deputies should exercise such leadership and develop it in others. Inspectors should look for evidence of it in schools. Leadership teams and heads should also review the use and allocation of time in schools to ensure as much time as possible is dedicated to allowing such leadership to take place. I know there is a lack of time in primary schools to release teachers; this has been the case for decades. However, whilst there may not be enough time, or as much as we would wish, this should not prevent us from doing what we can. Making time for learning-centred leadership to take place is something that should be a priority. Heads and others should examine how established time patterns might be changed to accommodate this form of leadership.

Learning-centred leadership occurs at six levels of learning

These are: pupil, teacher, staff, organisational, leadership and networks. When it occurs at all six levels, leaders will be closely in touch with what is happening in classrooms and there will be a high levels of 'hands-on' leadership. Also, everyone in the school will know that learning is what matters most in their school and that everyone will be striving to learn their way forward. Whilst the intensity of attention to classrooms will be quite different to the time – not so long ago – when hardly anyone visited colleagues' classrooms, the climate of such interaction will be developmental. Acknowledging colleagues' skills, strengths, developments and expertise will be hallmarks of learning-centred leadership.

Ensuring that leaders are knowledgeable about learning and teaching

In one sense the form of learning-centred leadership ensures that leaders – particularly those who do not teach as much as they once did – keep in touch. However, it will also be important that we have heads and others who can lead the change away from teaching as transmission to more constructivist forms of learning.

When several of the foregoing are combined they reinforce the importance of distributed leadership

Increasing the number of leaders increases the influence which can flow across the school and in and out of classrooms. We should also recognise and respond to the fact that there is just too much to know about learning and teaching for any single person to possess. No one has a monopoly on craft knowledge. Indeed, it needs to be co-constructed and transferred to colleagues. Distributed leadership means not only moving from the power of one to the power of everyone but also upping the power of everyone.

The long held belief in heroic leadership is no longer as good an idea as once thought

We need many more leaders, and we need them at all levels. This means that leadership is not necessarily confined to positional roles. Throughout this book I have presented leadership as being largely the property of organisational roles. This is why I have talked almost exclusively about heads, deputies and middle leaders. However, let me make it clear that I regard the move to distributed forms of leadership as a staged process. At present the shift is under way from believing only in head teachers to a belief in deputies, middle leaders and teams as well. Yet caught up in this shift is also the possibility that when learning-centred leaders identify colleagues with skills and strengths which others should appreciate and adopt and encourage the teacher to develop colleagues accordingly, then we also move into teacher or peer leadership. When this begins to happen on a regular basis and is effective, schools will have moved beyond the frame of positional leadership. Nor should leadership be confined to teachers, administrators and support staff also exercise leadership. The main point, though, is that leadership changes from being fixed to something which is more fluid and emergent.

Leadership becomes more flexible and fluid a feature in the school

As this happens so too will individuals need to be able to enact the twinned roles of leader and follower. At one time you might be leading; at others you might be following someone else's lead. Everyone will need to learn to be a leader, but we all might need to learn to be a follower too. Followership involves those accustomed to leading – for example, heads and deputies – letting go. This is not always easy to do and may take some individuals time to get used to. Equally, distributed leadership means others need to take hold of leadership opportunities when these are offered or made available to them. How this will all work out is difficult to say, because it will take on many complexions, not least because a great deal will depend on the particular contexts. In some schools, letting go and taking hold will not be problematic; in others it could be. However, if all the other conditions – particularly a school climate characterised by openness, trust and security – are present, I would expect leaders to grow in confidence because their followers will be understanding, supportive and willing them to succeed.

8   Overview and conclusions

In this chapter I shall review the main themes which emerge from the research findings and my discussion and interpretation of them. The intention is to summarise the key points and then to highlight what these imply for leadership in primary schools. The chapter is organised into four sections. In the first I present the common themes from the research into leadership in small, medium-sized and large schools. In the second I discuss how leaders influence classroom practice. I argue that this is a major theme in the book and one of central importance to the success of leaders and their schools. In the third section I explain what all of the foregoing means for colleagues who move from small to larger schools. In the fourth section I discuss what these findings mean for leadership in primary schools. This discussion develops my belief that leadership in primary schools is changing.

Themes in the research findings

This book is based on the premise that context matters. Throughout the book I have demonstrated that leadership is strongly influenced by the context in which it is exercised.

Context, though, is a rather more complex notion than is often appreciated. The most obvious sense of context for school leaders is the organizational one. The schools they lead are of great interest and fascination to them. When heads and other leaders talk to one another they usually focus on the school as an organisation, describing: how well the school is performing; its size; whether the school roll is increasing, declining or stable; the social and economic factors which impinge upon the pupils and their parents; the quality of teaching and so on. The school as an organisational context for the work of leaders is complex. It requires leaders to deal with multiple variables which combine and interrelate in subtle and shifting ways so that leaders must always be watchful and aware of what is happening.

However, increasingly, context also includes national, educational policy-making. The English education system has developed into both a centralised and decentralised one in recent years. The curriculum and assessment systems are determined centrally, while schools manage their own finances and staffing arrangements and are responsible for the quality of teaching and learning. Such arrangements mean that as national policies are formulated and implemented school leaders need to understand them and to know what is expected of them. Schools are no longer immune from external forces. Indeed, it is questionable if they ever were. However, today it is even more important that leaders are aware of what policymakers are thinking and planning.

In this book I have concentrated on one aspect of context: the size of the school. This is not to deny that there are many others, as I have acknowledged above. Nevertheless, I have argued that size makes a difference to the nature of the school, its organisation and its leadership. In Chapters 2, 3 and 4 I illustrate how this manifests itself.

In small schools, successful heads are active and engaged with what is happening across the school and in every classroom. They are hands-on leaders involving themselves in seemingly everything in the school. They are observant and sensitive to all that is going on around them. As enquiring leaders they not only note what is happening but analyse what they see and hear and then synthesise this information to make sense of it. They are hard-working individuals with an appetite and capacity for work. Moreover, they know it is important to do this because they wish to lead by example. Leading by example involves many things, but it certainly includes pulling one's weight and being prepared to do the same tasks as everyone else.

While much of a head's role in small schools involves them personally, this is not to say they rely entirely on themselves. Successful leaders also design and use a range of school structures and systems to support themselves and sustain the work of the school. This finding was equally apparent in medium-sized schools. Here, the leaders did most of what was observed in the small schools, but the heads in medium-sized schools placed a stronger emphasis on the structures and systems than did their counterparts in smaller schools.

Structures and systems are both the background and foreground to leadership. They provide organisational stability and create certainty and common procedures because they form the ground rules for everyone. Yet they are also the 'tools' of leadership. Systems for observing classrooms, communicating with staff, parents and governors and methods for analysing and evaluating the school's performance and development are ways in which leaders draw attention to issues and concerns. Leaders can choose from all the systems that are in place which ones to focus on. In this way leaders select those issues, interests and priorities which they believe all the staff should attend to. Furthermore, the way in which particular issues are addressed can be circumscribed by the principles of procedure inherent in the structures and systems. For example, classroom observation systems could be heavy-handed forms of 'checking up' on colleagues making staff feel they are under surveillance. By contrast, in the studied schools, classroom observation was a vehicle for teacher and staff development because there was an emphasis on positive, constructive feedback, peer observation and teacher development.

It was also apparent in the medium-sized schools that the heads, like those in the small schools, were strongly person-centred leaders. They placed a premium on interpersonal skills and dealt with colleagues on a one-to-one basis. They valued personal contact and behaved sensitively towards all they encountered. Yet they were also determined leaders, many being driven by a powerful need to succeed. They were also willing to share their leadership with others, notably the deputy head but also members of the school's management and leadership team.

This mix of individual and shared leadership was even more pronounced in the large and very large schools. Here, a blend of shared and distributed leadership was evident. Deputies were close partners of the head, while in the largest schools assistant heads were also involved in working alongside the head. If heads, deputies and assistant heads demonstrated shared leadership, the deployment of heads of year and Key Stage or unit leaders revealed that there were many middle leaders too. These middle leaders showed that leadership was distributed in the larger schools. One feature of this distribution of leadership, though, was that it remained fastened to positional leadership.

At the NCSL we have been exploring the idea of distributed leadership. It is one of the propositions the College has adopted because it embodies the idea that schools should harness their human and social capital (NCSL 2001). Through work with middle leaders and desk studies into the literature we have noted that distributed leadership can take a number of forms. For example, research by Bennett *et al.* suggests there are three distinctive elements. Distributed leadership can be viewed as:

1   An emergent property of a group or network of interacting individuals – this contrasts with leadership as arising from an individual. It is to do with people working together, pooling their initiative and expertise so that the outcome is greater then the sum of their individual actions.
2   An opening up of the boundaries of leadership – thus it is not confined to 'senior leaders'. Much of the literature suggests that leadership is distributed to teachers, but there are other members of the school community whose roles need to be considered, including pupils.
3   Varieties of expertise are distributed across the many, not the few. Numerous capabilities reside in the individuals spread across the organisation and if these are brought together it is possible to forge a dynamic which is not only greater than the sum of their parts, but also initiated by individuals not formally thought of as leaders.

(see Bennett *et al.* 2003)

The first of these three forms of distribution suggests leadership is not confined to one person but can include members of a group, team or staff. Indeed, leadership could be thought of not as a characteristic of an individual but as a property of the group. The second suggests that leadership extends beyond the teaching group. The third is really a combination of the first two, suggesting that leadership can move beyond organisational position and be exercised by anyone in the organisation.

Given these distinctions it is no surprise that in recent years so much has appeared in the literature on the subject of leadership empowering others. Distributed leadership is about making others more powerful. It is about increasing the contribution of many more leaders and ensuring they are given the opportunity and support to lead.

The research into leadership in large schools also showed that there were many teams at work in them. The schools that were visited as part of the research consisted of year teams or units of teachers. This is a sensible tactic, not least because it enables members of the organisation to feel involved and keeps everything to a human scale. While teams are usually a good idea, when there are lots of them this poses another question: how are they connected with one another so that fragmentation and competition are avoided? It is important to forge links between the teams in order to ensure organisational cohesion and coherence. Teamwork was evident in smaller schools, but here great stress was placed on creating a sense of 'whole school'. In the smaller schools teamwork meant either the entire staff working as one team or bringing together staff who worked in two teams (typically Key Stage 1 and 2 teams). The heads of the larger schools also wanted a sense of 'whole school' but knew this had to be achieved by bringing all the teams together. Thus in large schools leaders need to be able to develop a sense of unity from among all the different units of the school.

Creating and sustaining a sense of 'whole school' is therefore more challenging in larger schools because it means bringing and keeping together many more teams of staff than in smaller schools. In other words, as the number of teams in a school increases, so too does the need to hold them together.

It follows from these discussions of teamwork and distributed leadership that leaders in large schools must be able to do two things. Firstly, they must be capable of dealing with organisational complexity. Organisational structures, teams and teamwork all need to be designed and developed so that staff are able to work productively both together and apart. In some ways, it might be said that leaders of large schools need a knowledge of structures which exceeds that of their colleagues in smaller schools. Secondly, they also need to be skilled at developing a number of other leaders in the school. These are two of the main differences between leading large and smaller schools.

Influencing classroom practice

The examination of the effects of school size upon leadership casts light on how leaders influence what happens in classrooms. In many ways this issue is the most important one in the book. Yet despite its importance, remarkably little work has been done on how leaders influence what happens in classrooms. Although we know that leaders definitely influence classroom practices, we do not know enough about how they do this. Therefore the discussion in Chapter 5, where I investigated this issue, makes a contribution to the development of our knowledge in this area.

In that chapter I discussed the notion of learning-centred leadership, which I described as resting on three strategies of influence: modelling; monitoring and dialogue. These three strategies appeal to both teachers and heads. Teachers say that when used effectively they find them highly beneficial, not least because they encourage them to learn about their teaching and to develop and strengthen their pedagogy and understanding of pupils. Heads, being teachers who have been promoted on the basis of their success as classroom practitioners, also know these strategies are influential and therefore adopt them.

I also argued, drawing upon the evidence from my own and others' research, that leaders exert influence in both direct and indirect ways and that they rely on personal, shared and distributed influence. As the size of the school changes these forms of influence alter so that in different-sized schools different patterns of influence can be detected. Simply stated, the emerging pattern is that the larger the school the more distributed leadership becomes, although this is not to suggest that the process does not, or cannot, occur in small schools.

Given this general pattern, the key issue is that what is distributed is not simply 'leadership' but *learning-centred leadership*. We need to increase the influence of all staff to support and shape the quality of teaching and learning across the school. Learning-centred leadership might at first be enacted by positional leaders – that is, colleagues who occupy particular organisational roles, such as heads, deputy heads and Key Stage leaders. Yet they in turn identify through their monitoring, dialogues and conferencing colleagues whose classroom and pedagogic practice is worthy of emulation by others. The process of observing staff and talking with them allows leaders to identify which individuals might offer pedagogic leadership to their colleagues. Thus distributed leadership moves from one to many more positional leaders and then to teacher leadership when they are invited to teach their peers.

The virtue of such distributed learning-centred leadership is that it ensures sufficient 'density' of leadership to change classroom practice. The power of one can sometimes move schools, but in order to sustain improvement and to transform schools we need a form of distributed leadership that is so frequent and regular that leaders are kept closely in touch with classrooms and that the processes of modelling, monitoring and talk become part of the school culture.

Therefore, heads and other senior leaders need to provide learning-centred leadership and be able to develop other leaders to exercise it. The bigger the school, the more senior leaders must develop others to do this and the less they may need to enact it themselves, although I would argue that all leaders need to exercise it for some of the time. Distributed, learning-centred leadership thus depends on heads and senior colleagues creating the conditions for learning-centred leadership development to take place in the school. It also depends on heads building learning-centred leadership capacity in the school. These two ideas go hand in hand.

Moving from small to larger schools

It follows from the foregoing that as heads move from small schools to larger ones the requirement upon them to develop staff – as teachers and as leaders – changes. In small schools, heads need to be able to develop teachers as teachers and continue to hone their own classroom skills and understandings. In medium-sized schools, where a head's teaching commitment is likely to be less intensive in terms of the time devoted to it, they need to be able to develop shared leadership, most obviously with their deputy, but, as the size of this group of schools increases, also with members of the SMT.

In the past much of this type of work has really been about sharing out management tasks. Management matters, as I have stated on several occasions, but not so much that no one other than the head exercises leadership. If the past was about delegated management, the future is about distributed leadership; which, given the foregoing sections, means learning-centred leadership. Heads should ensure they are developing and sustaining this particular form of leadership.

Therefore, as the size of the school increases, when leaders move from one size to another they need to recognise that they need to develop more and more learning-centred leaders. This involves them in mentoring and coaching new and inexperienced leaders and making sure others are prepared for these roles. The implications for deputies in large schools are obvious; indeed, this may mark a new and important departure for them. Instead of being managers of tasks and projects given to them by the head, they could become – as some already are – developers of middle leaders.

In addition to these changes, as heads move from smaller to larger schools they also need to be prepared to deal with the increased complexity of the school as an organisation. There are many aspects to this change, but here I shall address just one. As the size of the school increases, there are plainly many more people to work with and attend to. Moreover, the school will be divided into units and sections, each of which will have its own needs and perspectives, and each of which will want to keep the head informed of their views, knowledge and concerns. The lone leader can easily be overwhelmed by all the information that flows to them – there is just so much to take in. This is where the structures and systems (e.g. evaluation, data handling, reporting systems) can play their part in making what comes through manageable rather than too demanding. While it is important to keep the knowledge levels manageable, it is also vital to keep the knowledge flowing to leaders because this information is 'intelligence'. It is vital to know what is going on in the school. In large schools it may not always be possible to be a hands-on leader, but it is possible and vital that leaders keep in touch with what is happening.

It is vital because from all the different sources of knowledge the head and members of the leadership team receive, they must develop a 'big picture' of the school. It is imperative that leaders make sense of what is happening, know what this means for the school's progress and priorities and are able to describe the direction in which the school is going. This is not easy, and it is very easy to fall into the trap of what Fullan (1991) calls 'false clarity'. In other words, being too sure – or too premature – in forming a view.

It is vital to develop the 'big picture' because of the problem of parts and wholes. Everyone, including the head, will have a particular view of the school. Often this is based on a very partial knowledge of it, although it is not unusual for individuals to generalise from their particular perspectives and claim that the whole school is as they see their small portion of it! This state of affairs is best illustrated by the story of the blind men and the elephant, where by touching a part of the creature – a leg, the trunk, an ear, a flank – each believes they know what the whole is like. Heads must avoid holding a very limited perspective and should try to avoid being influenced by those who do. Heads will have their own particular perspectives, but these should not be partial. They must develop as rich, detailed and broad a portrait of the school as they can.

This discussion suggests there are two skill sets heads of larger schools need rather more than do those in smaller schools. The first is leadership-development skills. The second is data handling, information processing and sense-making. Here is not the place to delve deeply into either or both. Nor do I wish to suggest that heads in small schools do not need them, or that these are the only different ones. I simply want to note that in terms of the research reported here, these are the two for which there is an evidence base. To these two skill sets should be added a third, which was noted in the section highlighting the themes in the research. This was the need for heads of large schools to have a knowledge of organisational structures and for them to be able to design and develop organisational structures, teams and teamwork which sustain staff motivation and participation.

Leading primary schools

If the above summarises many of the key issues discussed in this book, what do these ideas mean for leadership in primary schools? What do they appear to be saying about leaders and leading primary schools? In this section I shall attempt to answer these questions.

It seems to me that the research reported and reviewed in this book implies that leadership in primary schools is changing; moreover, it looks set to change even more in the near future. For some time I have argued that headship in primary schools is concerned less with role changes and more with control by role continuities (Southworth 1999, 2002). Primary headship, as I discussed in Chapter 1, is largely about individuals who are pivotal, proprietal and powerful. Leadership is seen as individual – the head – and heads frequently see themselves as the paramount leaders. In some ways this is what attracts them to the role. As a head you can make a great deal of difference, more than any other post in the school allows. Also, the accountability structures sustain such a role. If we think leadership makes a difference, then when we visit or inspect a school we look to see if the leaders are making a difference. Beliefs can become self-fulfilling if we are not careful. They frame our perceptions so that we see what we know and this, in turn, obscures what other leaders might be doing.

However, there are signs – in the studies discussed in this volume and across the literature about primary schools – that the role of heads and other leaders is shifting. What can be detected here is a move away from the old pattern of lone leadership to something which is more shared than formerly. The vocabulary of the heads researched in the three studies was most interesting because it included such terms as leadership and management teams, partnerships with deputies and teamwork. Of course, a new language does not necessarily mean different behaviour. Yet there is sufficient evidence from the teachers and deputies I interviewed to suggest that the heads' claims were not fictional ones. However, the research samples reported here do not justify a sweeping generalisation. At best they indicate a movement at the leading edge of practice. This movement is away from heroic leadership and towards more inclusive forms.

Expressed another way, there may be less interest in the leader and more in leadership. Perhaps we are moving towards a hinge in the history of leadership and its development in primary schools. We may be at a turning point in leadership development, when the orthodoxy of being reliant on the head to be *the* leader may be beginning to soften and to be substituted by stronger emphases on leadership being a phenomenon which is spread across the whole school. It is difficult to attribute this shift to a specific cause. Probably a combination of factors are encouraging it. These include, in no particular order:

- The emphasis on distributed and shared leadership which has grown in recent years;
- Primary school traditions of teamwork and collaboration now informing the nature of leadership as well as steering the teacher cultures of many schools;
- Gender differences – there are now more women heads than men, and there are probably many more all-female staff groups than previously;
- The drive for improving schools and the focus on pedagogy compelling many heads to involve teacher colleagues more than otherwise to provide teacher leadership;
- The national literacy and numeracy strategies developing the confidence of subject leaders to influence the classroom practices of their colleagues;
- Increased levels of monitoring heightening some heads' awareness of teachers' talents and skills;
- A significant cohort of deputies who do not seek headship but who nevertheless want to perform a positive and fulfilling role;
- Growing interest in assessment for learning, accelerated learning, multiple intelligences, emotional intelligence and so on, encouraging heads to remain as learning-centred leaders and to foster teacher colleagues to do the same;
- Increased levels of school-based management causing some heads to supplement their leadership with that of others;

- Enhanced professional development provision for school leaders through Higher Education programmes, LEA courses and the NCSL's national programmes and development activities;
- The increasing emphasis on building leadership capacity in schools.

No doubt others could be added. However, my intention is not to present an exhaustive list, merely to illustrate some of the likely forces which may have prompted the shift. Nevertheless, what the list does convey is the fact that leadership might be changing because of a range of forces, not all of them necessarily exerted upon head teachers. Change is stimulated by many forces and comes from several different sources, including some unexpected ones.

If, then, there are grounds for arguing that primary school leadership is moving away, in some schools, from a monocular view of headship to a more widely based notion of leadership, what does this in turn mean for the nature of leadership in primary schools? I have suggested that it should be learning-centred, distributed and person-centred. At the same time, it should be leadership for learning and encourage leadership learning and growth. As we move towards more distributed patterns of leadership there will be a concomitant need to develop leaders. This process of development is best conducted in schools, although external support and advice available through local courses, national programmes, consultant leaders and access to communities and networks of leaders, such as the NCSL has created, will all have a part to play. Distributed and shared leadership will only thrive if schools take responsibility for growing their own leaders.

In reality that has always been the case, but today it is even more so. While individual heads have often been forces for good in many schools, there is always a danger that an individual places limits on what can be achieved. Charismatic leaders can be inspiring for some, but they can also create glass ceilings for others. I have always believed that two heads are better than one. Heads can be positive and powerful energy sources, but they can also leave deputies and teacher colleagues feeling underpowered. Schools prosper when the strengths, experiences and talents of all who work there are released and orchestrated.

The notion of orchestration can be used as a cautionary metaphor too. In the book 'The Maestro Myth' which examines the practices of orchestral conductors, Norman Lebrecht (1997) writes:

> The conductor exists because mankind demands a visible leader or, at the very least, an identifiable figurehead. His musical *raison d'etre* is altogether secondary to that function.
>
> He plays no instrument, produces no noise, yet conveys an image of music-making that is credible enough to let him take the rewards of applause away from those who actually created the sound.
>
> (Lebrecht 1997: 2)

There are analogies here with heads who neither teach nor exercise learning-centred leadership nor ensure others provide such leadership. More than anything, though, there are parallels with those heads who retain all the power and seek all the glory for themselves.

Although a note of caution has been sounded for many years about the concept of heroic leadership, today there is some evidence to suggest that while charismatic leaders can rescue ailing and failing organisations they are poor at sustaining sound and successful ones. In Chapter 6 I used the work of Collins (2001) to assess heroic leadership. I now want to return to this author's work because he argues that what organisations need in order to move from being good to great is Level 5 leadership.

Level 5 leaders are seemingly ordinary people quietly producing extraordinary results (Collins 2001: 28). They are driven, especially with a need to produce results (p. 30). They are tenacious and dogged, and their style includes hard work and great diligence (p. 33). They blend personal humility with professional will (p. 21). Perhaps two examples taken from Collins outline the nature of such leadership. First, their self-effacing natures:

> Level 5 leaders channel their ego needs away from themselves and into the larger goal of building a great company. It's not that Level 5 leaders have no ego or self-interest. Indeed, they are incredibly ambitious – but their ambition is first and foremost for the institution, not themselves.
>
> (p. 21)

Second, this emphasis on whether these leaders are egotistical or not prompts Collins to conclude that there are two categories of people. The first are ego-driven and cannot 'subjugate their egotistical needs to the greater ambition of building something larger and more lasting than themselves'. The second category of people can.

The leaders studied in this book are Level 5 leaders. Such leaders exist all around us, but because we have been fascinated by heroes and heroines for so long and because Level 5 leaders are modest, they do not step forward and we have not paid them enough attention. Now we need to find many more of them, and we need heads in schools to be looking for them and to develop them.

In some schools today there are leaders who look like Level 5 ones and who are looking for others to work with them. When they find them and develop them they will not only have moved their schools from good to great, but they will also have played their part in transforming the landscape of leadership in their schools and across the education system.

Such an outlook requires just one further thought. How Level 5 leadership plays out in a school will depend on that school's context and, in particular, on its size. Leadership in primary schools is contingent, in part, on the size of the school. That is what this book has shown and explained in more detail than has previously been attempted. We therefore always need to remember this when advocating a particular form or approach to leadership. Leadership matters – and so too does school size.

Appendix 1 Headship categories

The Hay Group, as part of their advice to the (then) DfEE on performance management conducted a category analysis of headship. They listed eighteen categories which were used in the HELP study (see Chapter 3) of leadership in medium-sized schools. The participating heads were invited to contrast their views about leadership with the eighteen items set out below:

1 Analytical thinking
2 Conceptual thinking
3 Confidence
4 Developing potential
5 Drive for improvement
6 Flexibility
7 Holding people accountable
8 Impact and influence
9 Information seeking
10 Initiative
11 Integrity
12 Leadership
13 Personal conviction
14 Respect for others
15 Social awareness
16 Team working
17 Tough, caring
18 Understanding others.

Appendix 2   Structures and systems in schools

The importance of structures and systems is discussed in Chapter 6. Here examples of the structures and systems used in four medium-sized schools are presented. The information was supplied by the heads of these schools when, as part of the HELP project, they were asked to report on the structures and systems they used under the following headings:

- Use of staff
- Planning
- Monitoring
- Use of evidence/data
- Use of meetings
- Training.

School 1

1 *Use of staff*

Strong management structure

- Senior management team (head plus two senior teachers) as opposed to head plus deputy;
- Identification of strong management personnel;
- Clear identification of roles and decision-making powers;
- All staff have clear, shared job descriptions with delegated functions;
- Staff recruitment is of the highest quality;
- Coordinators for all areas;
- High-profile assessment coordinator.

Strong non-teaching support

- All staff have clear, shared job descriptions with delegated functions;
- Planning collated weekly and termly and held centrally, coordinated by office manager;

- Support for parents' initial questions and concerns;
- Assessments collected and collated termly by office manager;
- Agenda and minute-taking for staff meetings and in-service training;
- Preparation of in-service and staff meeting resources;
- Teaching assistant time is deployed effectively to give maximum support;
- Resources ordered centrally – saves overlap.

SENCO

- Excellent practitioner;
- Clear job description and support systems;
- Office support for all Essex Stages meetings, moderation of Stage 3 and statementing process, implementation meetings, etc.;
- Support for individual education plans;
- Classroom support via teaching assistants.

General

- Staff development – all staff complete annual audit. Strengths/expertise share, weaknesses supported.
- Parent volunteer support in each classroom.
- Termly meetings and training for midday assistants, supporting behaviour management. Lunchtimes are pleasurable and constructive.
- Teachers are supported with behaviour management.
- Family learning: staff support literacy, numeracy and behaviour workshops.
- Staff extremely united and motivated.
- The school is an Investor in People and professional development portfolios are in use.
- Governor volunteers and responsible governors support staff at all levels.

2 *Planning mechanisms*

- School development plan is discussed with all staff and governors. All staff make a contribution.
- Coordinators complete subject audits on a rolling programmed driven by SDP.
- SDP is informed by teaching and non-teaching staff training and development audit.
- All coordinators complete action plans for their subject areas.
- All year-group leaders complete action plans for their year group.
- Head-teacher action plans to identify future development.
- SENCO action plans to identify future development.
- Assessment coordinator actions plans to identify future development.
- Staff development plan informs school development plan.

- School development plan is focused on improving teaching, learning and achievement.
- Class targets set by head teacher, class teacher and coordinators.
- Post-inspection action plan.
- In place: whole-school schemes of work and curriculum policies, assessment policy, record-keeping policy, marking policy, reporting policy, etc.
- Teachers have clear understanding of what they teach, ensured by in-service training and self-evaluation, and termly evaluation discussions with head teacher.

3 *Use of time*

- SENCO: Essex Stages meetings
  Observations
  Work sampling
  Working with individual children.
- Coordinators: release to audit and monitor subject areas
  Observations
  Work sampling.
- Year-group leaders:
  Peer observations
  Management meetings
  Staff development and appraisal
  Parent interviews
  Focused in-service training
  Assessment coordinators.

4 *Monitoring, evaluation and development strategies*

- Head teacher/SMT and coordinators monitor and review using classroom observations, work sampling, pupil and teacher interviews;
- Peer monitoring;
- Planning and evaluations monitored by head teacher, coordinators and year-group leaders;
- Head teacher, SENCO and class teacher use ESA meetings to monitor special needs;
- Able child coordinator monitors planning, work samples and oversees target-setting to ensure challenging tasks are set and IEPs are appropriate;
- Responsible governors monitor and evaluate by classroom observations, work-sampling and interviews with staff and pupils;
- Outcomes of evaluations are regularly reported to governors;
- Agreed changes that arise out of evaluations are incorporated into action plans and development plans;
- All action plans and development plans are monitored regularly.

5 *Use of evidence*

Evidence

- Baseline assessment informs termly and Year 2 targets;
- Use of Hertfordshire/Warwick fluency exit tests and Birmingham reading profiles to inform targets and track progress;
- NFER tests;
- Termly reading, writing, science and numeracy assessments;
- School improvement and value-added network;
- PANDA;
- Pupil self-evaluation data used to inform targets.

Use

- Individual pupils and cohorts are tracked using star systems/levels;
- Comparison of progress and attainment made against similar schools and national averages;
- Performance of boys and girls tracked and compared;
- Level 2C children to Level 2B;
- Data for summer-born children used for targets;
- Evidence used to target teaching assistant parental support;
- Comparison with national average;
- Analysis of termly progress made by individuals, classes and year groups to inform termly targets;
- Assessment data kept centrally and analysed to inform planning;
- Value-added data used to compare progress achieved which what might be expected;
- Performance data presented so that coordinators and governors are able to see trends and compare performances of boys/girls, able/less able in subjects and against similar schools;

6 *Use of finances*

- Financial management policy in which procedures and responsibilities are clearly defined;
- Governing body monitor finances following statutory requirements;
- SEN allocations for learning support are clearly defined and allocated appropriately;
- Each member of staff is a budget holder with responsibility for monitoring their own budget;
- Budget holders make financial bids for extra allocations;
- Budgets are given priority in line with the school development plan;
- Administrative support is well resourced and appropriate finances allocated;

- Learning support is given a high priority and is well resourced and targeted to areas of greatest need – this is evaluated and revised regularly to ensure effective use.

7 *Use of meetings*

- All formal meetings have agendas and are minuted by the office manager;
- All formal meetings have set start and finish times;
- All documentation for meetings prepared by office manager;
- Weekly staff INSET meetings for all staff where appropriate;
- Meetings led by all staff including non-teaching staff;
- Regular informal meetings with head teacher and office manager to discuss budget and other issues;
- Daily informal meetings of teach staff, head and non-teaching staff before school;
- Informal lunchtime meetings;
- Termly meetings with midday assistants to discuss future strategies for lunchtime;
- Termly full governing body and committee meetings;
- Termly parent evenings to discuss and set individual pupil targets;
- Termly Essex Stages meetings to discuss IEPs with SENCO, head teacher, class teacher and parents;
- Summer term pre-school entry meetings with head teacher and new parents to discuss children's entry into school;
- 'Open door' policy for parents and staff so that problems are dealt with immediately and informally;
- Emphasis on informality – we are talking all the time.

School 2

1 *Use of staff*

Importance of having curriculum coordinators with clear responsibilities. All teachers have at least one curriculum area, except NQTs. Each has a clear job description, with clear expectations. These expectations are regularly reinforced at staff meetings.

Size of school and two buildings mean two Key Stage coordinators. They are responsible for the day-to-day issues at the respective Key Stage/building. One is SENCO and the other responsible for mentoring and early years issues.

The head and deputy and Key Stage coordinators are joined in the management team by the assessment coordinator (previously a +2 but now part-time and +1) and by the maths and ICT coordinator (+2).

The deputy head is literacy coordinator, at present, and staff development manager. The management team together organise the timetables of the LSAs, and the deputy head meets with them during assembly time once a week. There are two levels of LSA: those who are experienced and have been trained, and more recent recruits. The midday staff are led by a senior assistant who attends the lSA meetings. There are two office staff: the traditional secretary and finance technician. The finance technician, in particular, takes a lot of responsibility.

The site manager has their own budget but clears major repairs, etc. through the school office (i.e. finance technician and head).

When first appointed I used +1 as quality circle leaders to lead teams – including non-teaching staff – to establish aims and policies.

Time

I try to spend as much time as possible out of the office during school hours, but my availability to do this varies.

Most frustrating aspect of time, is lack of finance to offer non-contact time. A large carry forward figure five years ago meant the ability to give non-contact time at an important time in the school's improvement. That money is no longer available, and present development is held back by the ability to offer only minimal time. The future looks bleak with the implications of the new Essex formula coordinators have been given ideas for carrying out their monitoring role without non-contact time, and I am able to give some cover, but more time would make a big difference to school development.

One of the changes that have taken place is the amount of time teachers are expected to teach, and the amount of time we expect children to be on task.

2 *Planning*

A two-year long-term plan has been in place for the last few years, regularly revised following changes in requirements re foundation subjects, and the introduction of the literacy and numeracy strategies.

Medium-term plans are produced by teams termly, and the subject plans given to coordinators for monitoring and evaluation. The comments are given to Key Stage coordinators, who produced a report for information and action.

Lesson plans are produced for all lessons with samples given to coordinators. A standard format is used for medium- and short-term plans.

3 *Monitoring*

As part of our teaching and learning policy, teachers can expect to have their teaching monitored through head teacher observation once every half-term. I also monitor the attitude and behaviour of particular children, and this also provides the opportunity to observe teaching.

4 *Use of data*

Data is increasingly used to set expectations.

In terms of SATs results, national, local and 'similar school' comparisons have been made for some time.

The progress of all children is tracked using SATs results, statutory and non statutory, teacher assessment, reading ages. This also aids the target-setting process. I hold a copy of all these results. I will flag up the names of any children whose progress gives me concern.

As long as end of Key Stage results improve, they give teachers a boost. There is a concern about results reaching a plateau.

5 *Use of meetings*

Monday: – Management meeting. Used for diary planning, but also strategic planning.

Tuesday – Opportunity for parents to meet with teachers.

Wednesday and Thursday – Staff meeting. Used for curriculum planning, writing, refining policies. Teams meet for curriculum planning. Many lessons are planned jointly.

School 3

1 *Use of staff*

- Try to employ for the year, the float teacher, which is usually the deputy head, helps with monitoring, mentoring NQT/QTS, observations, SENCO, acting as head EAZ project leader, organising TA support, covering classes. This helps with supply costs, courses, illness. Enables a saving to allow her to have time off in the third term.
- There are three year-group leaders. They organise weekly meetings. They have their own year-group leader's job description. One of them is the deputy head. The other two are the more senior staff who act as acting deputy head when I am out. They share this role (agreed by them). We don't have senior meetings as there are only a few left out and this seemed inappropriate in a culture of sharing.
- The TAs now work in every classroom during every morning. This covers the numeracy and literacy hours. They now see all the children during the week. They work from the class plans. This also enables the teacher to work with every group and therefore have a good understanding of every child's needs from SEN/IEPs to the more able child.
- We have employed TAs to work with individual children (statements), behaviour support, catch up work with small groups, display.
- Our voluntary help is also targeted at individual children and they help with mini catch-up programmes.
- The office staff are highly trained, organised and supportive. They are up to date with current software e.g. optical reader for attendance, Internet, LTM5, school fund manager.

2 *Planning*

- The SDP is developed by all. Teaching and non-teaching staff, caretaker, cleaners, governors, middays. A day is organised as a workshop and four areas are discussed, i.e. management, curriculum, school environment, community. The budget is discussed in full.
- Curriculum planning is weekly. Led by the year-group leader. The staff plan to our long-term plans, devised by curriculum coordinators to address outcomes from the NC, which have been agreed by the staff.
- SCITTS trainees sit in on the planning sessions from day one. Their input is appreciated. Helps them to become familiar with the planning before their teaching practice. (Lots of fresh ideas.)
- All teaching staff write action plans for their own subject area. They also are in groups i.e. the arts, science, humanities so they can support each other.
- The deputy head and myself regularly write action plans and take items off that plan as equals/or experience. The deputy head is regularly put into the position of head whilst I am doing NPQH training or EAZ activities. She does lead while I am there. She has specific roles, e.g. SENCO, parenting skills groups, ERR research project, but staff often see her as leader even when I'm in the room.

3 *Monitoring*

- Copies of weekly plans are kept in the staff room for all staff to monitor (either as year group leaders, subject coordinators or management).
- We have a very extensive classroom observation timetable. *All* staff (TAs, teachers, head, deputy and SENCO) observing each other, Coordinators observing their subject, observing SCITTS or NQT or QTS or PGCE.
- GWA is another opportunity for all staff to monitor work produced by the children (Good Work Assembly).
- Staff also monitor work produced in their year group. Samples taken to weekly meetings.
- Head makes many unannounced visits to classes. This is made easier by the fact that we are open-plan. The one outside, demountable class produces a different situation as they know of my presence instantly.
- Staff meetings also give us the opportunity to monitor policies/schemes/planning sheets/assessment documents, etc.
- The governors have input from all staff in curriculum areas, management issues, premises issues. They visit and observe in classes. They inspect buildings. They are presented with regular finance updates.
- Individual targets, year-group targets, staff targets (from observations).

4 *Use of evidence/data*

- All staff examine data such as PANDA reports, OFSTED reports, Baseline data, EAZ data, test results, reading scores. This forms a basis of our development plans.
- We are involved in many research projects and data from these projects is also examined, e.g. Early Reading Research.
- Attendance/punctuality figures form a basis for our attendance targets.

5 *Use of meetings*

- SDP meetings with all. One of the best strategies we have adopted for that feeling of 'teamwork'.
- Regular weekly staff meetings where we all devise the timetable of events and everyone has the opportunity to lead. All TAs are also welcome and dip in and out.
- Weekly year-group planning for continuity, progression.
- I must admit that often we don't have a paper agenda, just a heading, and who is leading and what equipment/resources are needed. Someone always takes minutes, though, and these are kept in the staffroom for anyone absent, governors, TAs.
- All staff are able to contribute to the EAZ meetings.
- I seem to attend a tremendous amount. I am getting a little choosy lately.
- TAs have led meetings – one is leading the project of Essex Behaviour Award.

6 *Training*

- We try to create a lifelong learning atmosphere.
- We studied the best approaches to training. We now organise a very varied staff development plan including, county course, EAZ courses, advisers coming into school to lead discussions/workshops, advisers working in classes both teaching and offering advice, staff co-training each other, visits to others, others observing us, research reading.
- I am involved in NPQH training.
- Parents are involved in training, ICT, parenting skills, numeracy/literacy hour, handwriting, curriculum workshops.

School 4

1 *Use of staff*

- Movement of staff between year groups (at least every two years);
- Support staff who move through the school attached to a cohort;

- Whenever possible SENCO teaches the Easter/January intake so that during her 'floating' term she can teach special needs pupils, get on top of the paperwork and provide release time for colleagues;
- Deputy has regular release time to engage in management duties (half a day per week);
- Some specialist teaching at Key Stage 2;
- Clear handbook for teachers and CAs and a second handbook for MDAs.

2 *Use of time*

- Allocation of time to NC subjects, RE and PSHE, agreed and adhered to;
- Teachers produce timetables showing when each subject is being taught.
- Timetables for release time and monitoring sessions as well as room use and duty rotas.
- Organising my own free time effectively – termly time plan (including catch up weeks!), weekly timetable with tasks allocated to days/times (does not always work!).
- Providing some release time for all teachers each term – even if it is only half a day!
- I have learnt to delegate and say NO!
- Spending one evening a week reading – I never have time to read anything longer than single sheets of A4 at school.
- Keeping at least one day at the weekend free from school work for the sake of my mental health.

3 *Planning*

- Long- and medium-term plans in place for all subject;
- Planning files for each year group containing medium-term plans? Scheme of work;
- Agreed common planning format for weekly plans and half-termly overview;
- Weekly plans handed to head teacher every Monday morning;
- Subject managers involved in monitoring planning;
- Whole staff involved in formulation and review of school development plan;
- Subject managers set targets for the development of their subject area and bid for resources;
- Staff development is planned on an annual basis.

4 *Monitoring*

- Clear system in place;
- Termly timetable of head teacher monitoring sessions agreed;
- Head teacher monitors planning, teaching (formal and informal observations), samples of pupils' work, test results and assessments (both formative and summative);

- Subject managers monitor all of the above areas;
- Performance reviews carried out with all new staff;
- Professional development interviews annually with all staff (leading towards performance management);
- Deputy monitors success of INSET.

5 *Use of evidence/data*

- Database to track pupil performance;
- Baseline, LARR, SATS, Birmingham reading records, reading tests for special needs pupils and teacher assessment based on star system used to provide statistics.

6 *Use of meetings*

- Times of meetings negotiated with staff;
- Staff meeting agenda published termly;
- Development meeting – weekly after school, staff lead meetings as appropriate;
- Development meetings address needs identified in SDP;
- Business meeting – weekly, at lunchtime, cancelled if no urgent business;
- Support staff invited to all meetings.

References

Ainscow, M. Hopkins, D. Southworth, G. and West, M. (1994) *Creating the Conditions for School Improvement*, London: Fulton.

Allday, D. (1998) *Spinning Straw into Gold: Managing Intellectual Capital Effectively*, London: Institute of Management.

Bennett, N., Harvey, J., Wise, C., and Woods, P. (2003) *Desk Study of Distributed Leadership*, Nottingham, National College for School Leadership.

Bolman, L. and Deal, T. (1991) *Reframing Organizations*, San Francisco: Jossey-Bass.

Collins, J. (2001) *From Good to Great*, London: Random House.

Cotton, K. (1997) *School Size, School Climate and Student Performance*, Northwest Regional Educational Laboratory, School Improvement Research Series. http://www.nwrel.org/scpd/sirs/10/c020.htm.

Coulson, A.A. (1976). 'The role of the primary head', Reprinted in Bush, T., Glatter, R., Goodey, J. and Riches, C. (eds.) (1980) *Approaches to School Management*, London: Harper & Row.

Day, C., Harris, A., Hadfield, M., Tolley, H. and Beresford, J. (2000) *Leading Schools in Times of Change*, Buckingham, UK: Open University.

Deal, T. and Kennedy, A. (1982) *Corporate Cultures: The Rites and Rituals of Corporate Life*, London: Penguin.

Deal, T. and Peterson, K. (1999) *Shaping School Culture: The Heart of Leadership*, San Francisco: Jossey-Bass.

DfEE (1997) *From Targets to Action*, London: Department for Education and Employment.

DfES (2000) *Statistics of Education: School Workforce in England (including teachers' pay for England and Wales)*, London: DfES.

Dudley, P. (1990) 'Primary schools and pupil data' in Southworth, G. and Lincoln, P., (eds.) *Supporting Improving Primary Schools*, Ch. 4: 87–106, London: RoutledgeFalmer.

Dunning, G. (1993) 'Managing the small primary school: The problem role of the teaching head', *Educational Management and Administration*, 21(2): 79–89.

Elmore, R. (2000) *Building a New Structure For School Leadership*, Albert Shanker Institute.

Esmée Fairbairn Foundation (2001) *Heads You Win: The Report*, London: Esmée Fairbairn Foundation.

Fullan, M. (1991) *The New Meaning of Educational Change*, London: Cassell.

Fullan, M. (1993) *Change Forces*, London: Falmer.

Fullan (1999) *Change Forces: The Sequel*, London: Falmer.

Fullan, M. and Hargreaves, A. (1992) *What's Worth Fighting For in Your School?*, Buckingham: Open University Press.

Galton, M. (1995) *Crisis in the Primary Classroom*, London: Fulton.

Galton, M. and Patrick, H. (1993) *The Small Primary School*, London: Routledge.

Gittins (1967) *Primary Education in Wales – The Gittins Report*, London: HMSO.

Glatter, R. (1998) 'From struggling to juggling: towards a redefinition of the field of educational leadership and management', paper presented at the fourth ESRC seminar, 'Redefining Educational Management', October, Liverpool.

Gronn, P. (2000) 'Distributed Properties: A new architecture for leadership', keynote paper presented at BEMAS Research Conference 2000, Robinson College, University of Cambridge.

Hall, V. and Southworth, G. (1997) 'Headship: state of the art review', *School Leadership and Management*, 17(2): 151–170.

Hallinger, P. and Heck, R. (1997) 'Exploring the principal's contribution to school effectiveness', *School Effectiveness and School Improvement*, 8(4): 1–35.

Hallinger, P. and Heck, R. (1999) 'Can leadership enhance school effectiveness?' Bush, T., Bell, L., Bolam, R., Glatter, R. and Ribbins, P. (eds.) *Educational Management: Redefining Theory, Policy and Practice*, Ch.14: 178–190, London: Paul Chapman.

Hargreaves, A. (1994) *Changing Teachers, Changing Times*, London: Cassell.

Hargreaves, D. (1998) *Creative Professionalism: The Role of Teachers in the Knowledge Society*, London: Demos.

Hargreaves, D.H. (2001) 'A capital theory of school effectiveness and improvement', *British Educational Research Journal*, 27(4): 487–503.

Hayes, D. (1996) 'Aspiration, perspiration and reputation: idealism and self-preservation in small school primary headship', *Cambridge Journal of Education*, 26(3): 379–389.

Hersey, P. and Blanchard, K. (1982) *Management of Organisational Behaviour: Utilising Human Resources*, Englewood Cliffs, NJ: Prentice Hall.

Hill, P. (2001) 'What principals need to know about teaching and learning', paper prepared for the NCSL Think Tank, University of Melbourne.

HMI (1999) 'Small schools: how well are they doing?' *Primary School Manager* (May/June): 14–16.

House of Commons (1998) 'The role of headteachers', Education and Employment Committee report of proceedings, vol. 1, London: Stationery Office.

Huberman, M. (1992) 'Critical introduction' in Fullan, M., *Successful School Improvement*: 1–20, Buckingham: Open University Press.

Lebrecht, N. (1997) *The Maestro Myth: Great Conductors in Pursuit of Power* (Second edn), London: Simon & Schuster.

Leithwood, K., Jantzi, D. and Steinbach, R. (1998) 'Leadership and other conditions which foster organizational learning in schools', in Leithwood, K., and Louis, K.S. (eds.) *Organisational Learning in Schools*: 65–90, Abingdon, UK: Swets & Zeitlinger.

Leithwood, K. and Seashore Louis, K. (eds.) (1998) *Organisational Learning In Schools*, Abingdon, UK: Swets & Zeitlinger.

Leithwood, K., Jantzi, D. and Steinbach, R. (1999) *Changing Leadership for Changing Times*, Buckingham: Open University Press.

Little, J.W. (1981) 'The power of the organisational setting,' paper adapted from final report, 'School success and staff development,' Washington, DC: National Institute for Education.

MacBeath, J. (ed.) (1998) *Effective School Leadership: Responding to Change*, London: Paul Chapman.

MacBeath, J. and Myers, K. (1999) *Effective School Leaders*, London: Prentice Hall.

MacGilchrist, B., Mortimore, P., Savage, J. and Beresford, J. (1995) *Planning Matters*, London: Paul Chapman.

Mezirow, J. (2000) *Learning as Transformation*, San Francisco: Jossey-Bass.

Mortimore, P., Sammons, P., Stoll, L., Lewis, D. and Ecob, R. (1988) *School Matters: The Junior Years*. Wells, UK: Open Books.

National Commission on Education (1996) *Success Against the Odds*, London: Routledge.

NCSL (2001) 'Think Tank' report to governing council, National College for School Leadership, Nottingham.

Nias, J., Southworth, G. and Yeomans, R. (1989) *Staff Relationships in the Primary School: A Study of School Cultures*, London: Cassell.

Nias, J. Southworth, G. and Campbell, P. (1992) *Whole School Curriculum Development in Primary Schools*, London: Falmer.

Nonaka, I. and Takeuchi, H. (1995) *The Knowledge Creating Company*, Oxford: Oxford University Press.

OFSTED (1996) *Setting Targets to Raise Standards: A Survey of Good Practice*, London: Office for Standards in Education.

OFSTED (1998) *School Evaluation Matters*, London: Office for Standards in Education.

Rosenholtz, S. (1989) *Teacher's Workplace: The social organisation of schools*, New York: Teachers' College Press.

Schein, E.H. (1985) *Organisational Culture and Leadership*, San Francisco: Jossey-Bass.

Scottish Education Department (1990) *Effective Primary Schools: a report by HM Inspectors of Schools*, Edinburgh: HMSO.

Senge, P. (1990) *The Fifth Discipline: The Art and Practice of the Learning Organization*, London: Random House.

Sheppard, B. (1996) 'Exploring the transformative nature of instructional leadership' *The Alberta Journal of Educational Research*, 42(4): 325–344.

Southworth, G. (1994) 'Headteachers and deputy heads: Partners and Cultural Leaders' in Southworth, G. (ed.) *Readings in Primary School Development*: 28–55, London: Falmer.

Southworth, G. (1995) *Looking into Primary Headship: A Research-Based Interpretation*, London: Falmer.

Southworth, G. (1996) 'Improving primary schools: shifting the emphasis and clarifying the focus', *School Organisation*, 16(3): 263–280.

Southworth, G. (1997) 'Primary headship and leadership,' Ch.3, in Crawford, M., Kydd, L. and Riches, C. (eds.) *Leadership and Teams in Educational Management*, Ch.3, Buckingham: Open University.

Southworth, G. (1998) *Leading Improving Primary Schools: The work of headteachers and deputy heads*, London: Falmer.

Southworth, G. (1999) 'Continuities and changes in primary headship' in Bush, T., Bell, L., Bolam, R., Glatter, R. and Ribbins, P. (eds.) *Educational Management: Redefining Theory, Policy and Practice*: 43–58, London: Paul Chapman.

Southworth, G. and Conner, C. (1999) *Managing Improving Primary Schools*, London: RoutledgeFalmer.

Southworth, G. and Lincoln, P. (eds.) (1999) *Supporting Improving Primary Schools*, London: Falmer.

Southworth, G. (2000) 'How primary schools learn', *Research Papers in Education*, 15(3): 275–291.

Southworth, G. (2002) 'School leadership in English schools: Portraits, puzzles and identity,' in Walker, A. and Dimmock, C. (eds.) *School Leadership and Administration: Adopting a cultural perspective*: 187–204, London: RoutledgeFalmer.

Stewart, T. (1998) *Intellectual Capital: The New Wealth of Organisations*, London: Nicholas Brealey.

Turner, D. (1998) *Liberating Leadership: A Manager's Guide to the New Leadership*, London: Industrial Society.

Wallace, M. (1988) 'Innovation for all: Management development in small primary schools', *Educational Management and Administration*, 16(1): 15–24.

Wallace, M. and Huckman, L. (1999) *Senior Management Teams in Primary Schools*, London: Routledge.

Waugh, D. (1999) 'Talking heads: How have headteachers in primary schools of different sizes responded to education changes?', *Curriculum*, 20(1): 18–33.

Weindling, D. (1999) 'Stages of headship' in Bush, T., Bell, L., Bolam, R., Glatter, R. and Ribbins, P., *Educational Management: Redefining Theory, Policy and Practice*: 90–101, London: Paul Chapman.

Whitaker, P. (1997) *Primary Schools and the Future*, Buckingham, UK: Open University.

Woods, R. (2002) *Enchanted Heads*, Nottingham: National College for School Leadership.

Index

Ainscow, M. *et al.* 128

Bennett, N. *et al.* 160
Birmingham project 129–30
Blase, J.and Blase, J. 105, 106–8

classroom practice 159, 163; consistency in 137; influences on 161; and learning-centred leadership 161–2; maintaining contact with 149–50; modelling 34–5, 46, 104, 146; monitoring 33–4, 35, 36, 46, 53, 57, 62, 104–5, 121–2, 123, 146; professional dialogue/discussion 46, 105–9; tactics for influencing 41–2, 90–1, 98–101, 103–8, 112–13, 114–15, 124
collaborative culture 19, 57, 66–7, 126–7, 128–9, 130, 137, 147–8
Collins, J. 63, 120, 167
context 22–3; awareness of 54; complexity of 8; concept of 7; contingency/situational theories 8; culture/performance levels 7; dynamic aspect 8–9; factors involved in 7–8; ignoring of 1; importance of 1–2, 18, 54, 56, 158–9; national/international dimension 9; school/local dimension 9
Cotton, K. 15–16
Coulson, A.A. 89

Day, C. *et al.* 18, 28
Deal, T., and Kennedy, A. 61; and Peterson, K. 61
deputy heads 22, 127, 160; and delegation 86; enjoyment of work 85; interpersonal relationships 86, 88; leadership development 142–3; learning opportunity 84; preparation for 86–7; professional development 87; responsibilities of 86, 88; role of 70; teaching/administration mix 86; time management 87; views of 85–8; wish to become heads 87; working with heads 87–8
developing leaders/leadership 45, 92, 114; capacity 150–4; deputy head-teacher 142–3, 155; head-teacher 32–3, 48, 71, 83–5, 89–90, 91, 140–2, 155; learning-centred 144–50, 156; lone 90; and management 84–5; on-the-job learning 83–4, 139, 154–5; patterns of 89–90; shared/distributed 90; subject 143, 155–6; types 152–3, 156–7
distributed leadership 22, 151; achievement of 113; challenges belief in power of one 153; combination of individual/group 160; definition of 90; and delegation 37; elements 160; and empowerment 161, 162; importance of 156–7; in learning-centred organisation 162; move towards 166; notion of 152–3; and opening of boundaries 160; pattern for 113–14; as property of group 160
Dudley, P. 108
Dunning, G. 16

Early Reading Research Project 54, 63, 64
Education Action Zone 54
Elmore, R. 152–3
Esmée Fairbairn Foundation 49, 69
Essex Primary School Improvement (EPSI) Research and Development programme 54, 63–4, 129

Fullan, M. 102, 148, 164; and Hargreaves, A. 61, 127, 147